Sue and

I thought you both might
enjoy this. The good Doctor's
art is pretty cool, too.
Merry Christmas from Who-ville.

Much love,

The Secret Art of
Dr. Seuss

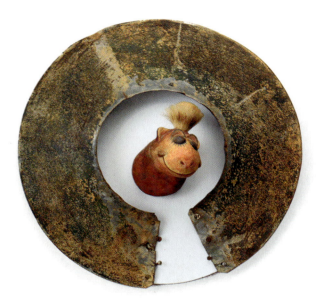

The Secret Art of

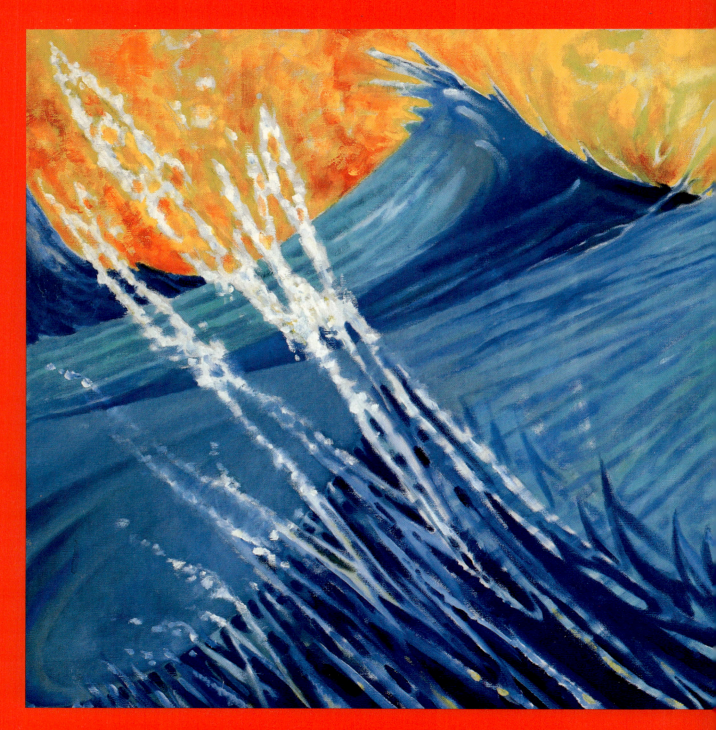

Dr. Seuss

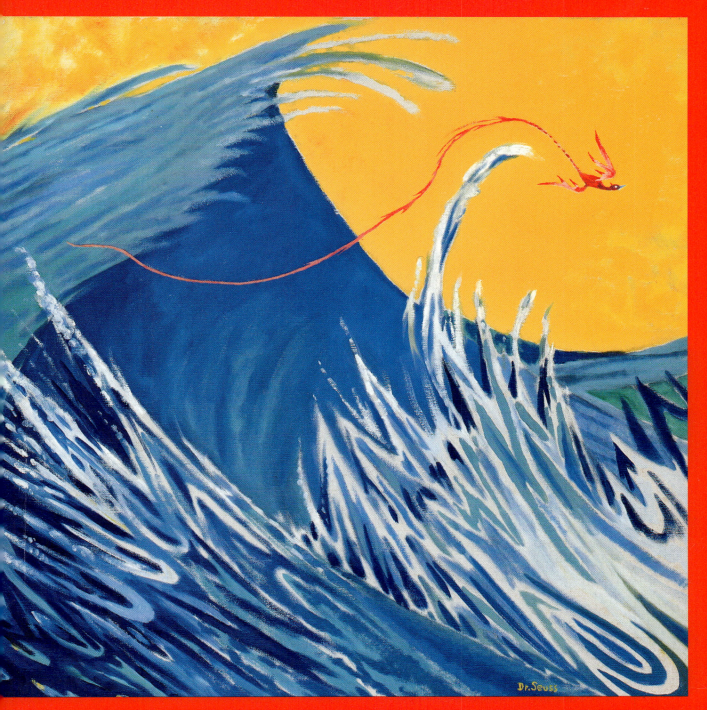

With an introduction by Maurice Sendak
Random House New York

Copyright © 1995 by Dr. Seuss Enterprises, L.P.
Introduction copyright © 1995 by Maurice Sendak

Photographs by Philipp Scholz Rittermann

Library of Congress Cataloging-in-Publication Data
Geisel, Theodor Seuss, 1904-1991
The secret art of Dr. Seuss / [author, Theodor Geisel] :
introduction by Maurice Sendak. — [1st ed.]
    p. cm.
ISBN 0-679-43448-8
1. Geisel, Theodor Seuss, 1904-198? — Catalogs. I.Title.
ND237.G325A4 1995
759. 13—dc20   95-19024
                                          CIP

Manufactured in the United States of America
98765432   24689753   23456789
First Edition

The Secret Art of
Dr. Seuss

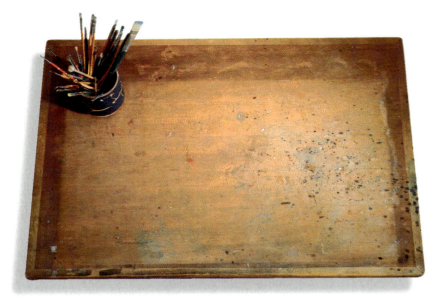

A PERSONAL NOTE ABOUT THEODOR SEUSS GEISEL by Audrey Geisel

I retain a most vivid picture of Ted standing in his studio before his easel, palette in hand, brush poised. He would lean forward and then back on his heels, head cocked to one side and then to the other. This artistic "dance" step was repeated over and over again.

He enjoyed working after midnight — seldom during the working-day hours. He did not consider painting to be "work," so it had to wait till late at night. Painting was what he did for himself and not something he felt comfortable in sharing.

I recall a particular oil painting — now known as "A Plethora of Cats" — in which there are dozens upon dozens of cat heads of all different sizes. There was never an actual moment he could feel he had indeed finished — that is, painted the last feline head. He would periodically step back and put it aside for a while. Then, inevitably, when the spirit again moved him — or he was on book hiatus — he would find room for just one more cat face. This happened over and over again. I have attempted to recall the very last cat face with special tenderness, but I cannot.

I remember telling Ted that there would come a day when many of his paintings would be seen and he would thus share with his fans another facet of himself — his *private* self. That day has come. I am glad.

La Jolla, California
May 1995

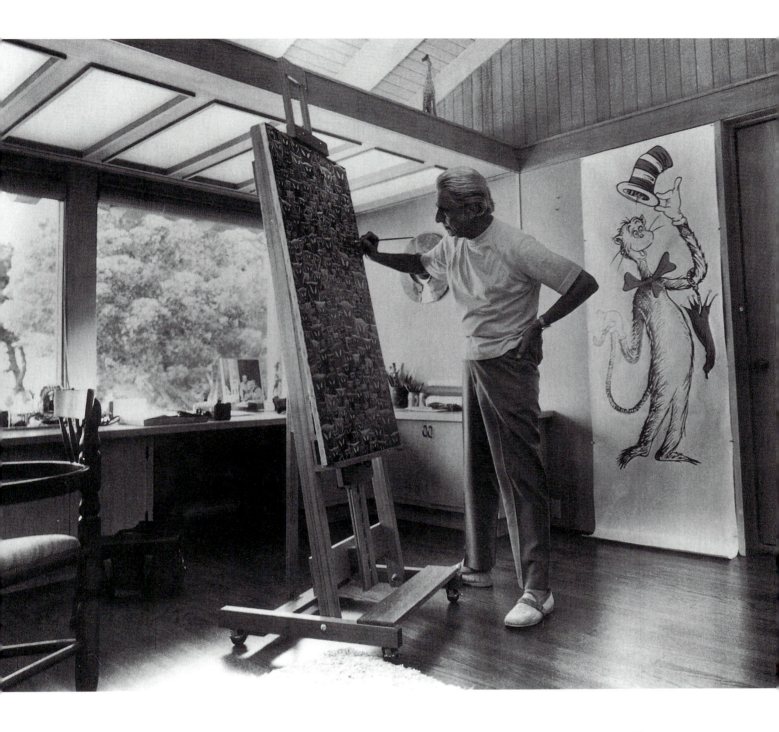

INTRODUCTION by Maurice Sendak

The Ted Geisel I knew was that rare amalgamation of genial gent and tomcat—a creature content with himself as animal and artist, and one who didn't give a lick or a spit for anyone's opinion, one way or another, of his work. He was, of course, immensely charming and polite about the whole matter, but when Ted fixed you with his calm cat-gaze, you knew when to shut up. It was easy to respect the simple modesty and curious privacy behind the gentle bluster of the man, but Seuss's apparent lack of interest in style, fashion, and any kind of analysis relating to his work astonished me. Only after years of friendship was I completely won over; Dr. Seuss was serious about not being "serious."

I loved Ted for his quiet, generous heart and genius. He had no difficulty lavishing praise on others and seeing himself—without false modesty—as your hardworking but ordinary craftsman. In that respect, he was much like Beatrix Potter, who, throughout her professional life, pooh-poohed the very high praise heaped upon her. In her old age, she bitterly denounced the business of children's books for belittling and patronizing children—thus the delight of knowing she had instantly claimed Seuss's *And to Think That I Saw It on Mulberry Street* a masterpiece. She recognized Seuss's genius and cherished his amazing simplicity and truthfulness. His lack of pretense allowed him to play and enjoy himself with gusto. That rare quality, combined with an uninhibited clarity of vision, produced some of the best books ever published for children.

Ted and I met years ago and liked each other immediately. I gave him reason to laugh mightily on more than one occasion when I launched into one of my "wacky" (his word) subtext theories relating to my favorite Seuss books. I was a product of fifties psychoanalysis, and he forgave me that and my terrible earnestness. Ted was magnanimous. He wondered, simply, how I could take his work so seriously. What I took seriously was the sheer pleasure of it all while pondering how he came spiritually unscathed through life, pleasure principle intact and infant joy forever gratified. It is that infant joy that makes Ted's work so deliciously subversive, and the watercolors, oils, and sculptures in this collection of his unpublished art only confirm his dedication to pleasing himself.

There was certainly nothing cookie-cutter, bland, or trendy about Ted Geisel. These works abound in nuttiness, "political incorrectness," and lots and lots of cats. In short, you have entered Seussville, where questions and doubts are left at the door with the coo-coo something-or-other. Enjoy yourself. The slippery, sloppery, curvy, altogether delicious Art Deco palazzos invite you to slide and bump along, in and out of flaming colored mazes (where serious cats lurk and hang about), and past grand, even apocalyptic, oceans and skies. The book is filled with fabulous geometric conundrums. Their milky, thirties movieland dippiness best conjures for me the private Seussian dreamscape: a Cat in the Hat theme park world, where loops and hoops and squares and limp bagel shapes, all charged with exotic color, have the demented nightmare effects provoked by a dinner of green eggs and ham. But the architecture—ah! the architecture—playing with a sensuous, loony physicality that re-creates the gleaming, rapturous infant domain, where various openings are to be seriously investigated and explored. All this tricked out with enormous technical panache: Seuss the Craftsman working hard to make you forget Seuss the crafts-man. The skill is in delineating a convincing and riveting dream. And so we dream Seuss dreams: a cat dream, finally. I counted at least twenty sneaky felines, but I suspect there are many more in disguise. Have a look at the fantastical "Cat Collecting Evidence in a Bad Part of Town" and tell me Ted Geisel wasn't one cool cat.

Ridgefield, Connecticut
May 1995

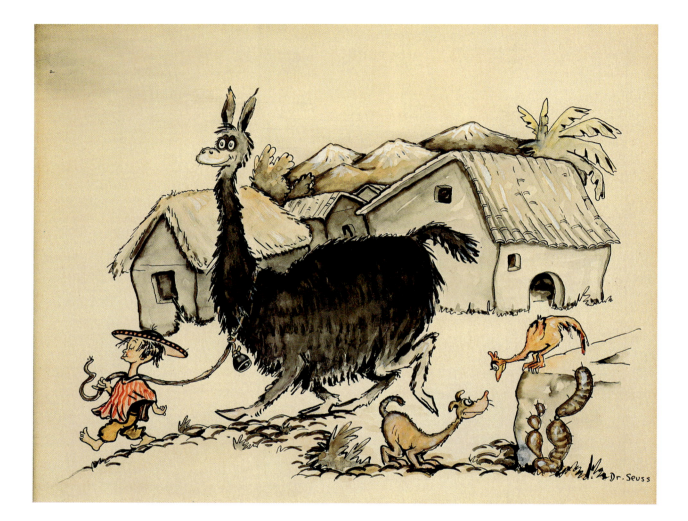

Peru I (Giant Llama Led Through Village) 1925

dimensions 10¼" x 13⅛"
media Pencil, ink, watercolor on bristol

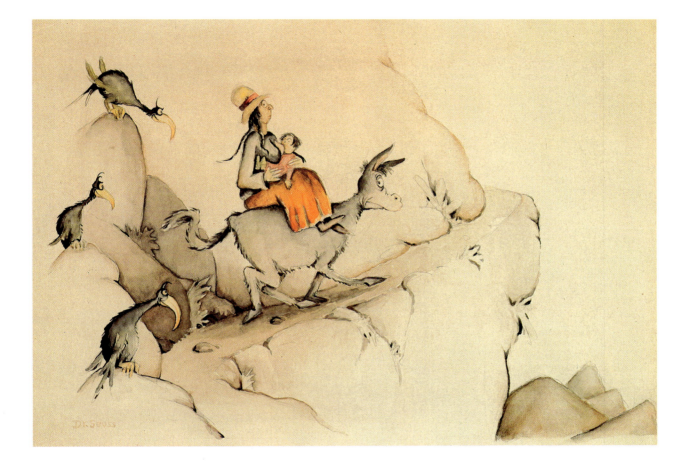

Peru 2 (Vultures Waiting for the Fall) 1925

dimensions 9⅞" x 15⅛"
media Pencil and watercolor on board

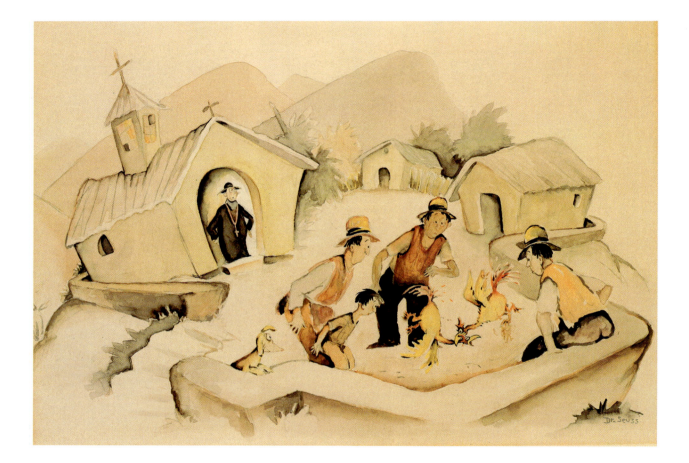

Peru 3 (Cock Fight) 1925

dimensions 9⅞" x 14⅞"
media Pencil and watercolor on illustration board

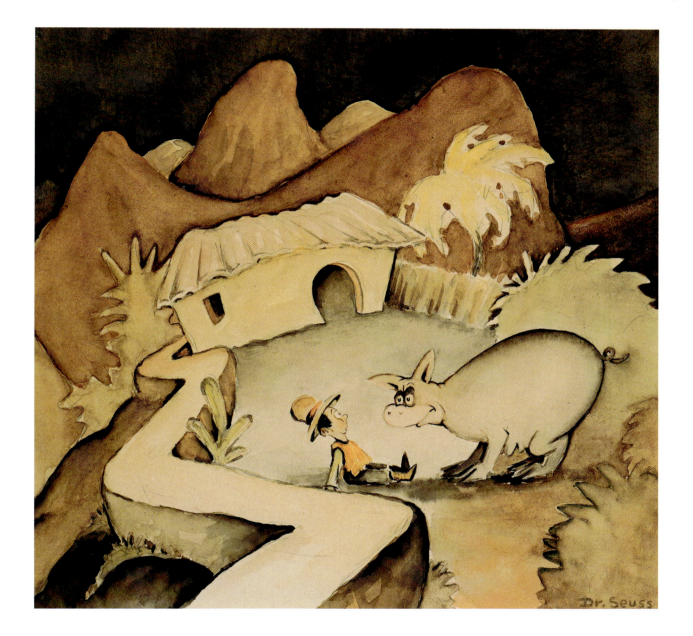

Peru 4 (Angry Pig) 1925

dimensions 9⅞" x 10¼"
media Pencil, ink, watercolor, on illustration board

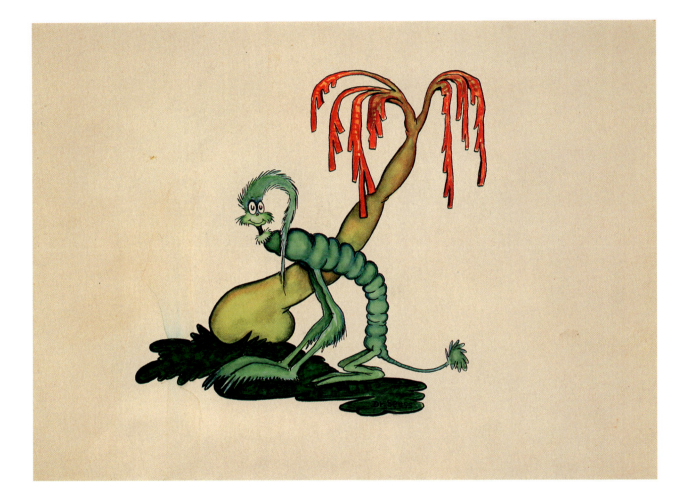

Zachery

dimensions 11⅛" x 14⅜"
media Ink and watercolor on paper

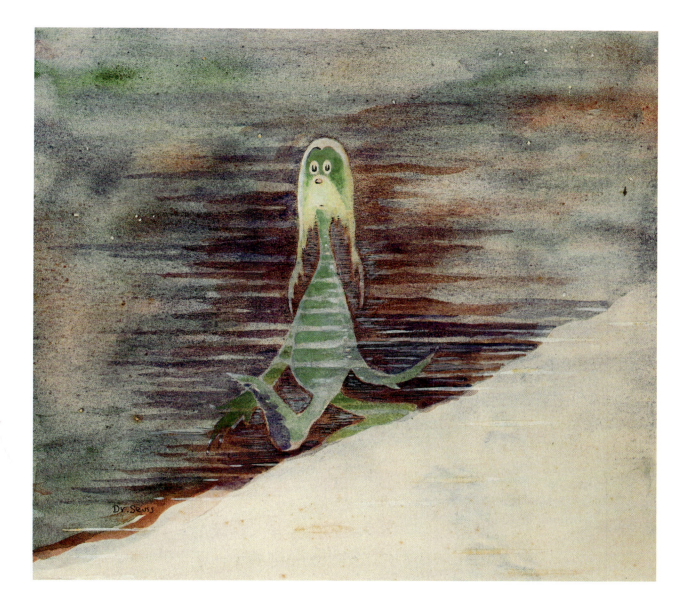

Spots

dimensions 9¼" x 10"
media Watercolor on board

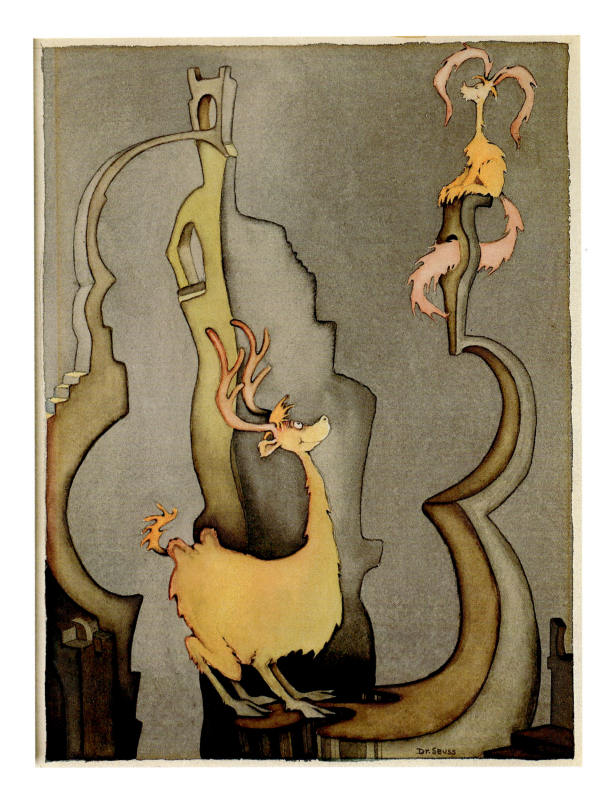

Antlered Animal Adoring Pink-Tufted Small Beast 1932

dimensions 16½" x 12⅜"
media Watercolor and ink on illustration board

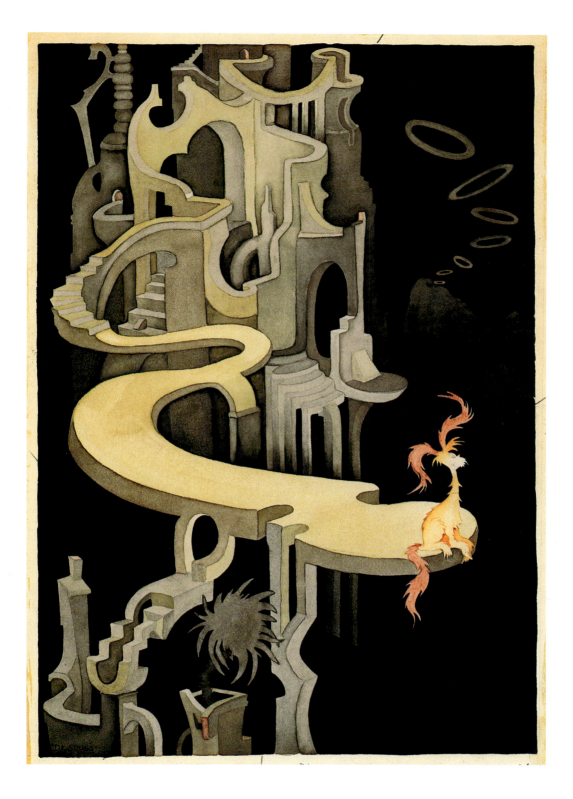

Pink-Tufted Small Beast in a Night Landscape 1960

dimensions 22" x 14¾"
media Ink and watercolor on illustration board

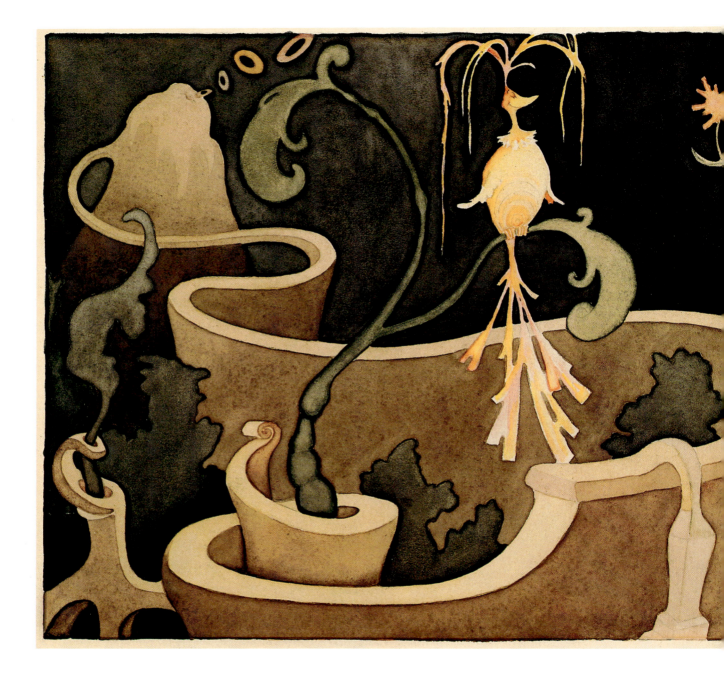

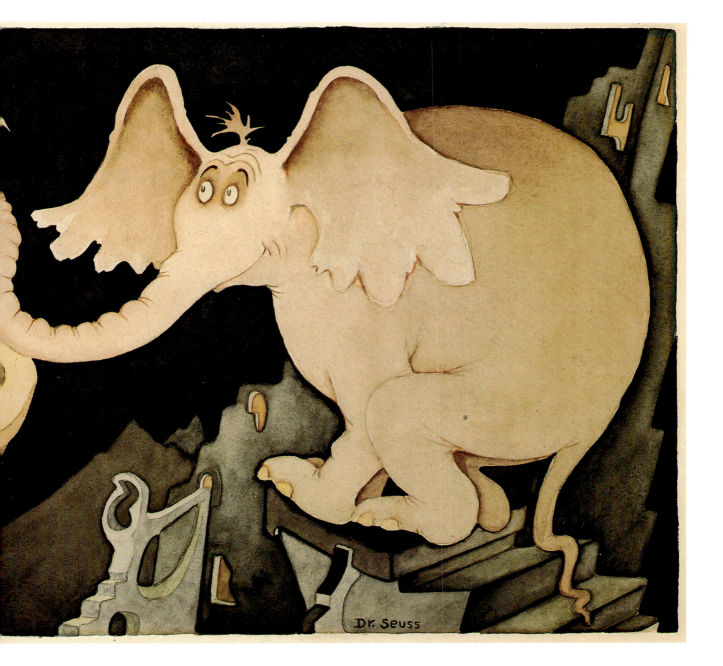

Elephant Presenting Flower to a Bird 1925

dimensions 14" x 26⅜"
media Ink and watercolor on illustration board

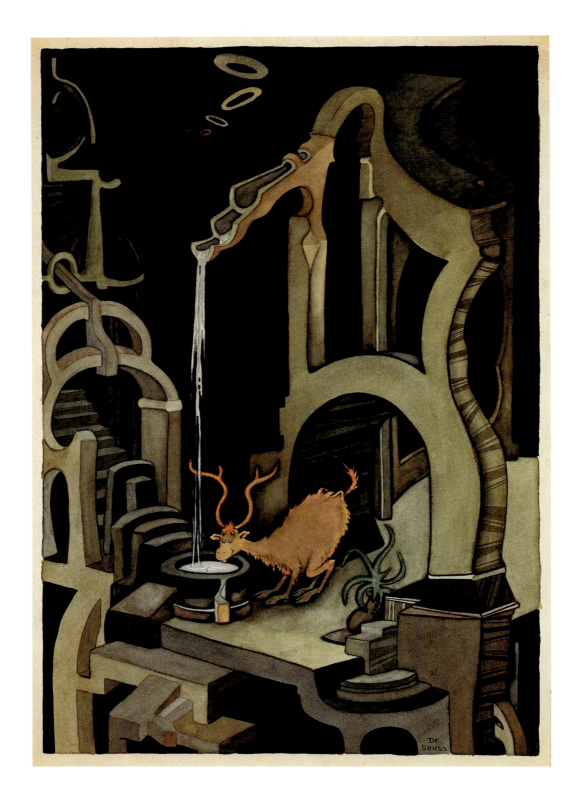

The Stag at Eve 1960

dimensions 22" x 15¼"
media Watercolor on board

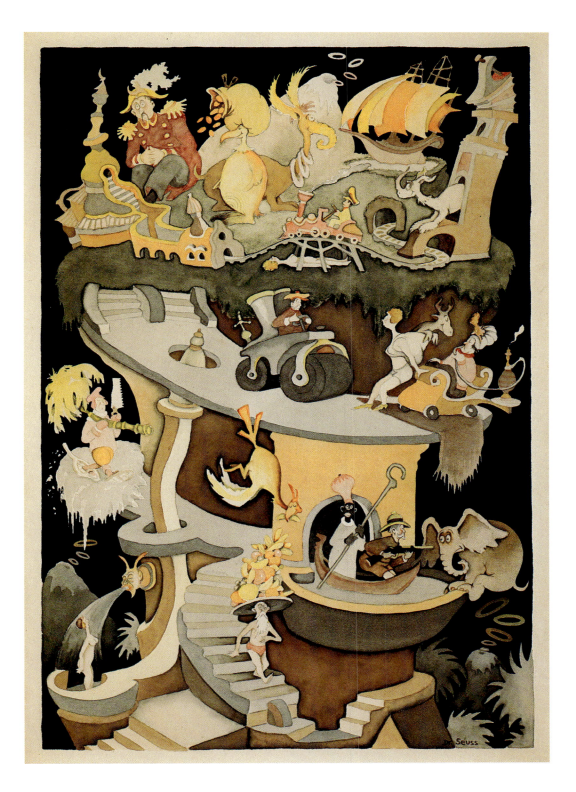

Tower of Babel

dimensions 20⅝" x 13⅝"
media Watercolor and ink on illustration board

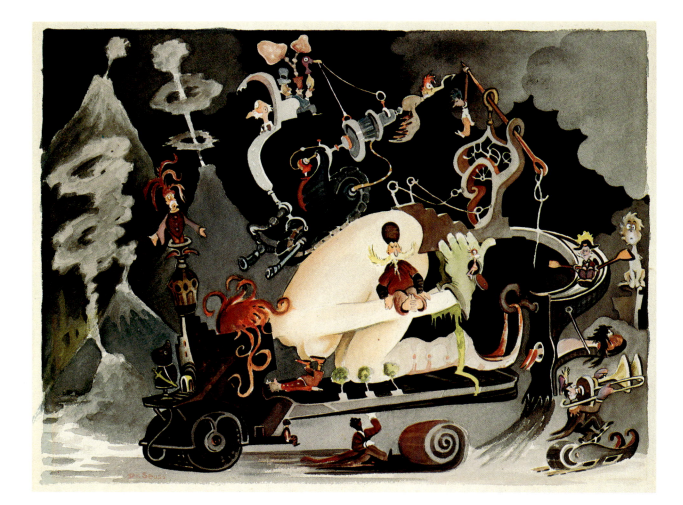

Untitled

dimensions 15" x 18¾"
media Ink, and watercolor on drawing board

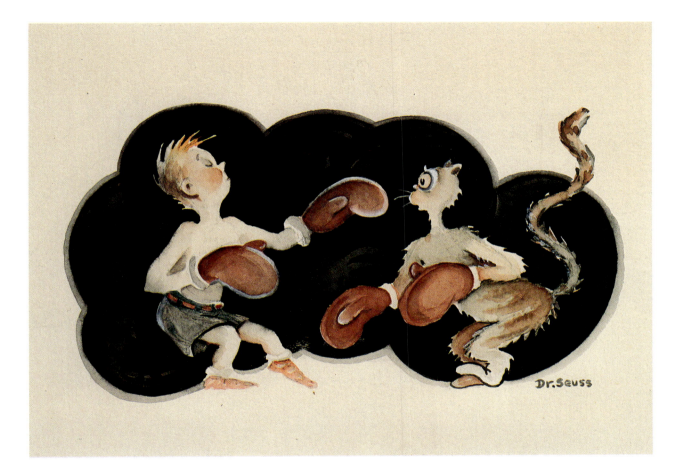

The Manly Art of Self-Defense 1927

dimensions 9¾" x 12½"
media Watercolor on board

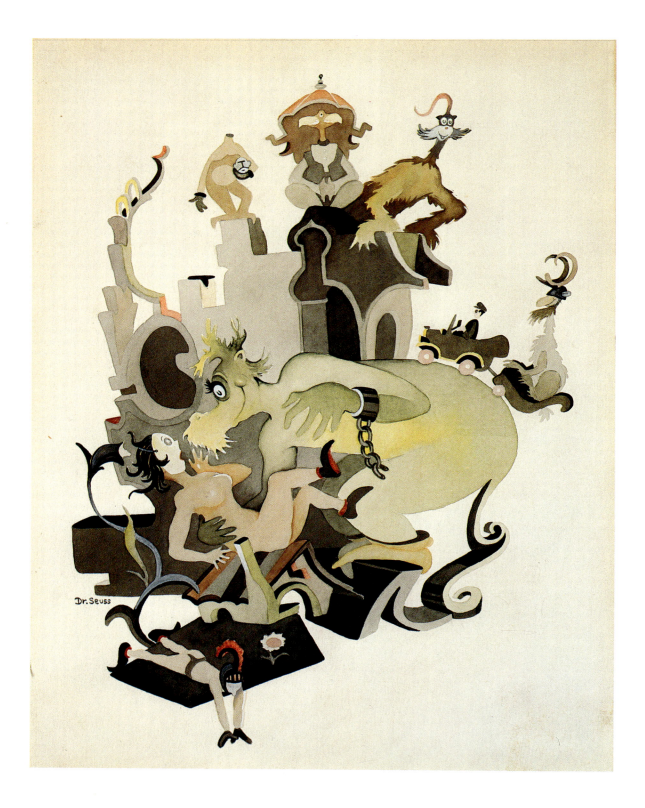

Untitled

dimensions 16⅛" x 12¼"
media Watercolor on watercolor board

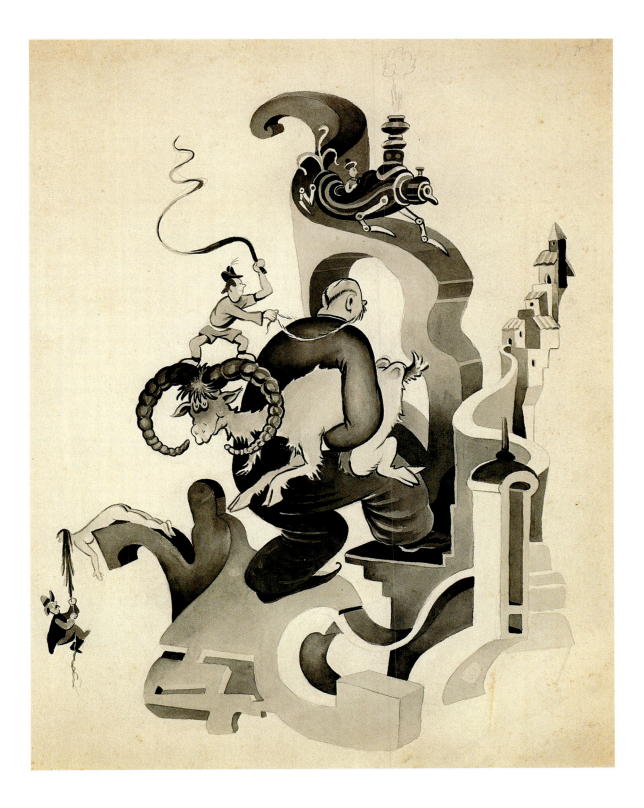

Untitled

dimensions 17¾" x 15½"
media Watercolor and pencil on illustration board

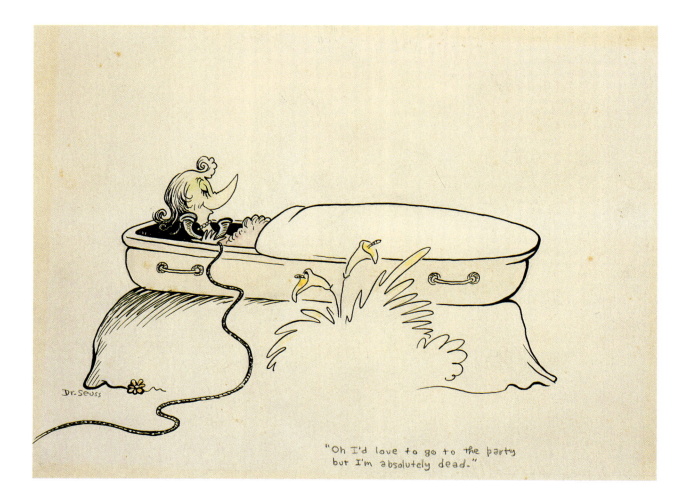

Oh, I'd Love to Go to the Party, But I'm Absolutely Dead

dimensions 11¾" x 14¼"
media Pencil, ink, watercolor on paper

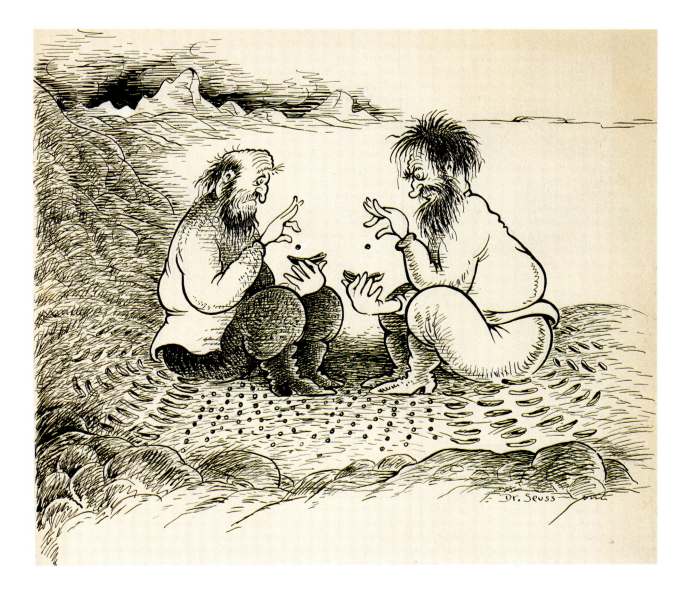

On the Steppes of Russia

dimensions 14" x 11⅛"
media Pencil and ink on paper

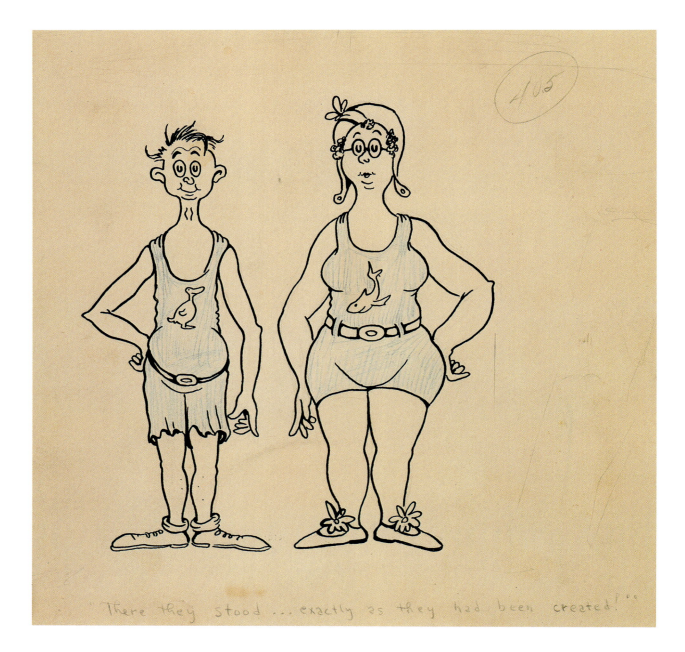

"There they stood ... exactly as they had been created!"

There They Stood Exactly as They Were Created

dimensions 10⅞" x 11¹⁄₁₆"
media Ink and colored pencil on bristol

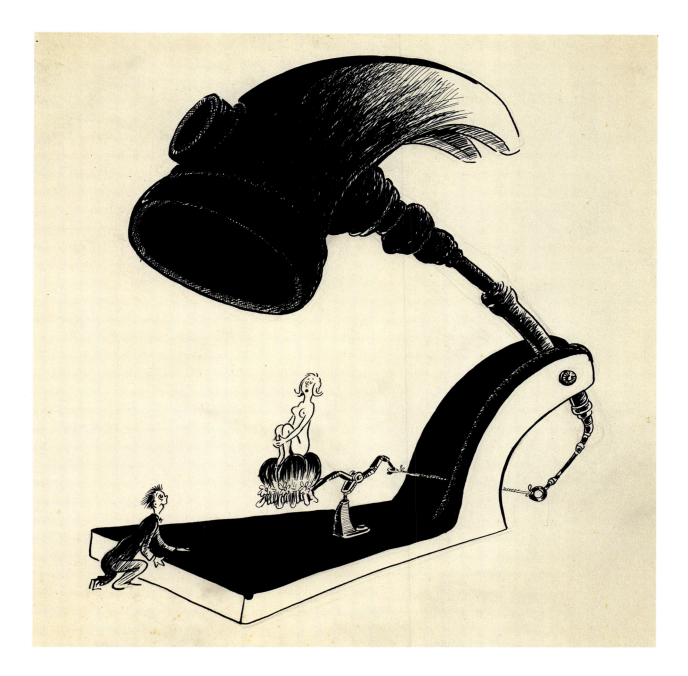

Untitled

dimensions 14½" x 13¾"
media Pen and ink and pencil on illustration board

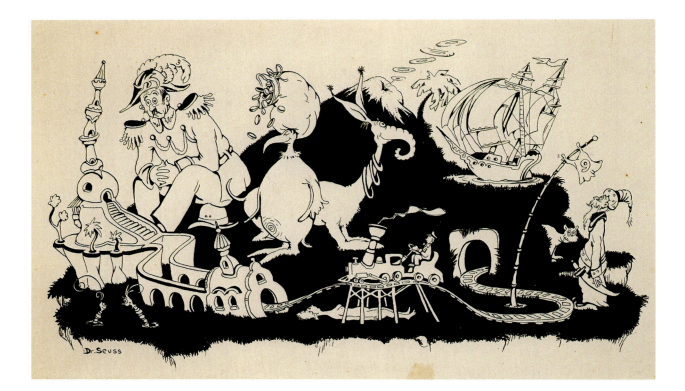

Landscape

dimensions 7½" x 12⅞"
media Pen and ink

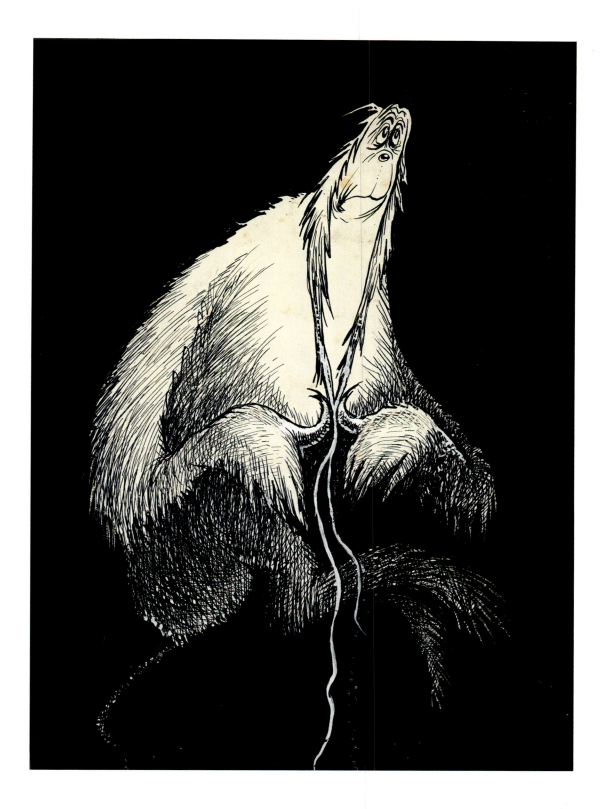

Self-Portrait of the Artist Worrying About His Next Book (reproduced in *Life* magazine) 1959

dimensions 12" x 16"
media Pen and ink, whiteout, oil pastel on board

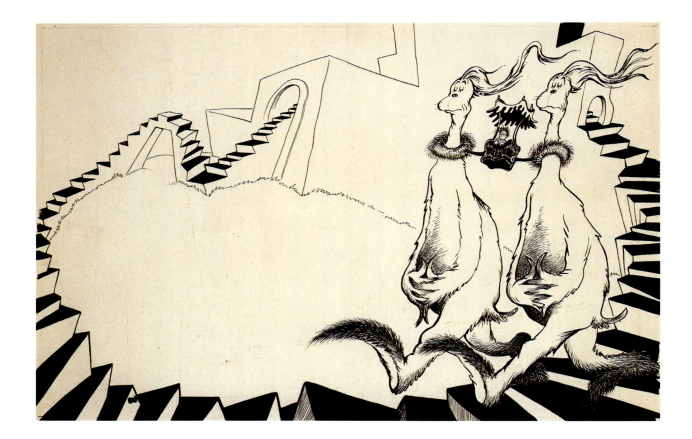

Taking Twin Heaslips for a Walk

dimensions 18⅝" x 26⅝"
media Pen and ink on bristol

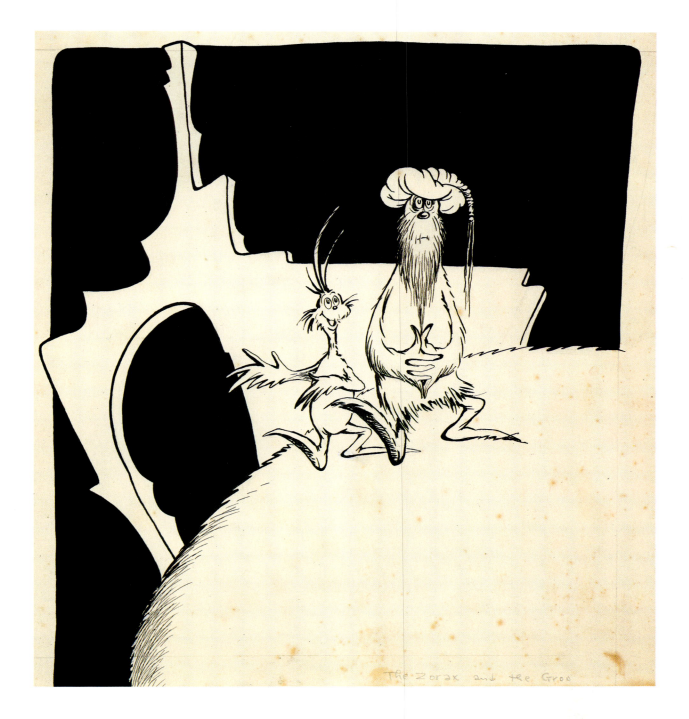

The Zorax and the Groo

The Zorax and the Groo

dimensions 13⅛" x 12"
media Pen and ink on illustration board

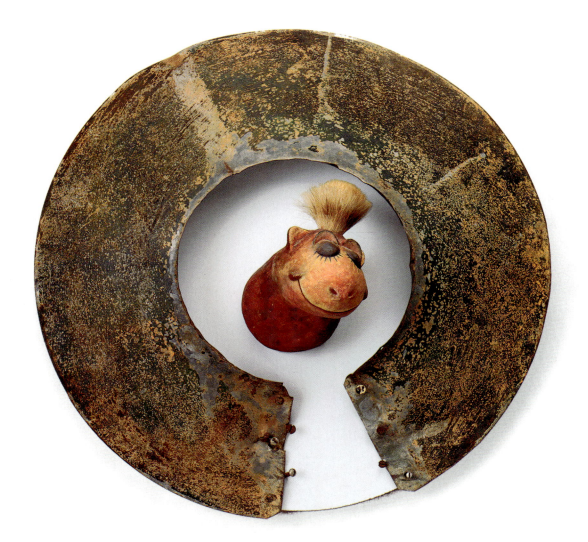

Tufted Gustard 1934

dimensions 19½" x 19½" x 6¼"
media Plaster, metal, screws, laminate, shaving brush on wood mount

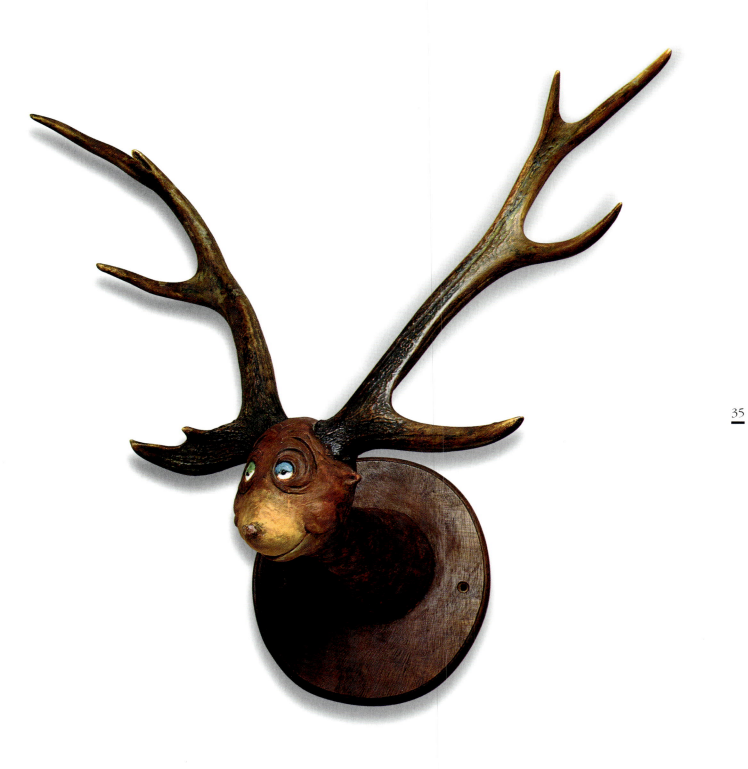

Semi-Normal Green-Lidded Fawn 1934

dimensions 22" x 16" x 10"
media Plaster, horns, oil on wood mount

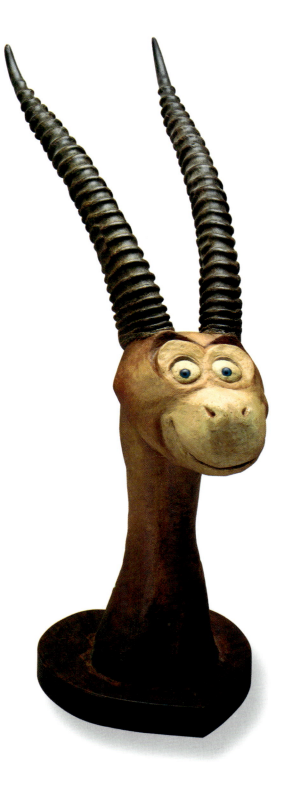

Two Horned Drouberhannis 1934

dimensions 17" x 6" x 16"
media Plaster, horn, oil on wood mount

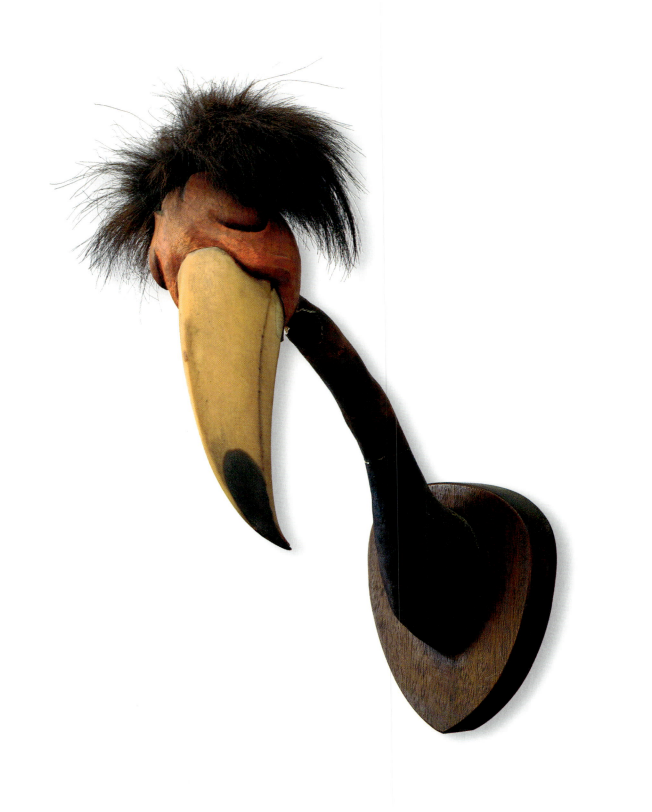

Andulovian Grackler 1934

dimensions 14" x 6" x 11"
media Plaster, fur, beak, oil on wood mount

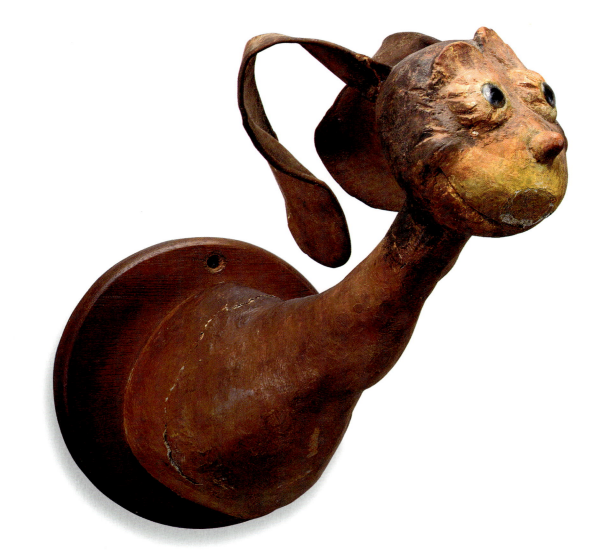

Seuss Animal (Anthony Drexel Goldfarb) 1934

dimensions 8½" x 5½" x 9"
media
Plaster, leather (rabbit ears), oil on wood mount,

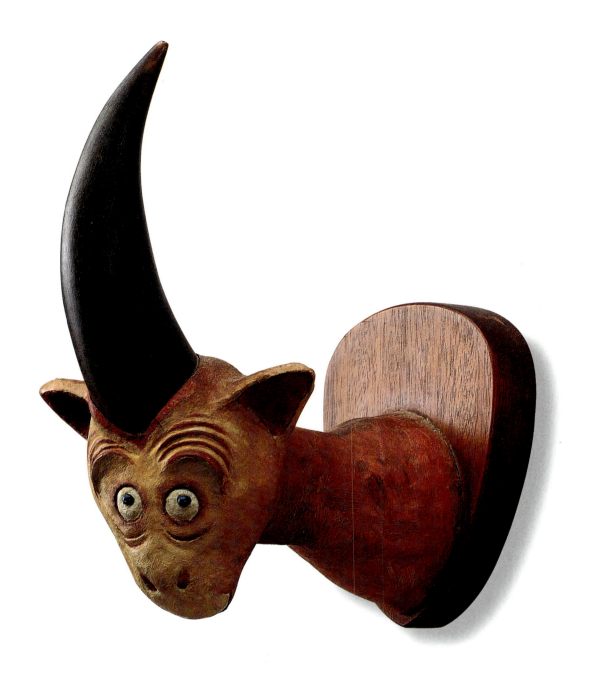

Mulberry Street Unicorn 1934

dimensions 8½" x 5" x 7½"
media Plaster, bull's horn, oil on wood mount

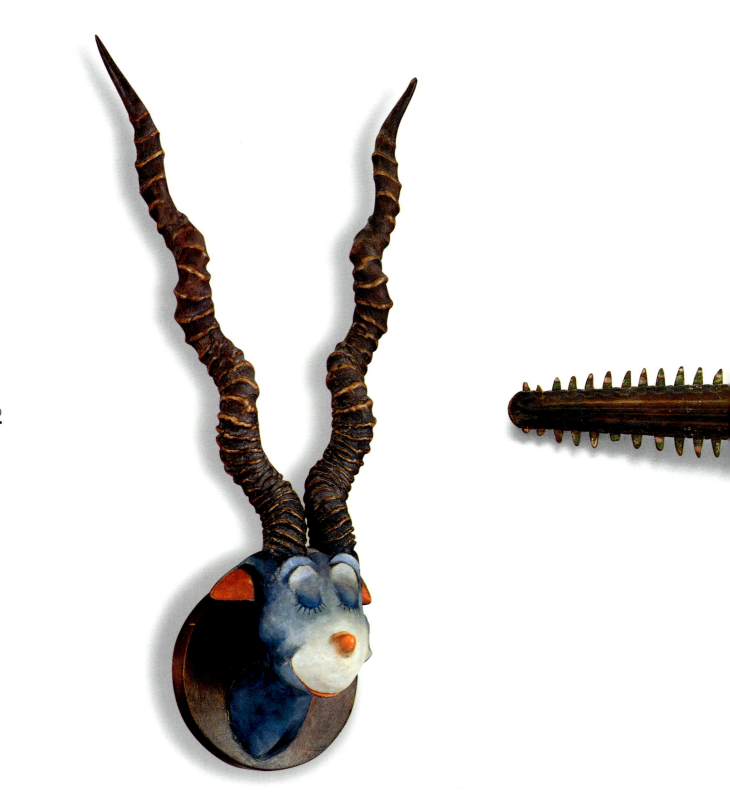

Blue-Green Abelard 1934

dimensions 24" x 12" x 6"
media Plaster, horns, oil on wood mount

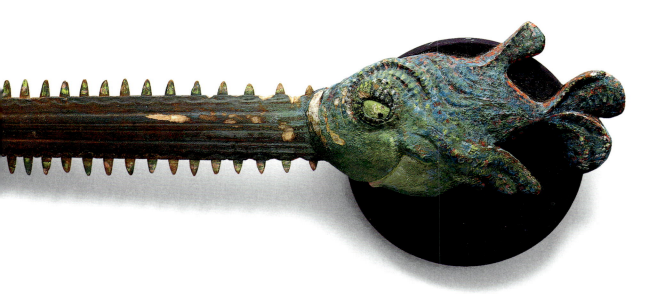

Seuss Sawfish (from *McElligot's Pool*)

dimensions 6" x 20½" x 2¼"
media Plaster, sawfish bill, oil on wood mount

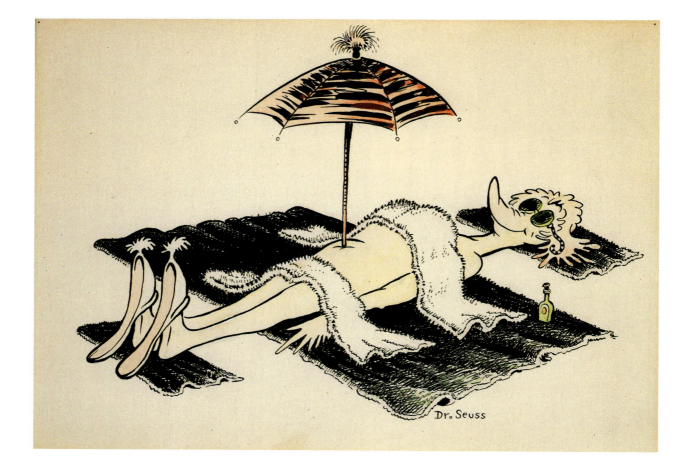

View from a Window of a Rented Beach Cottage (study)

dimensions 9½" x 13"
media Ink and watercolor on board

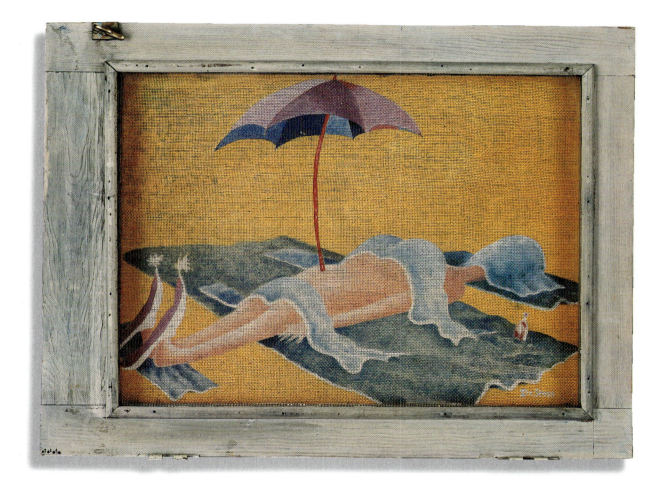

View from a Window of a Rented Beach Cottage

dimensions 17⅛" x 23½"
media Oil on board with hinged window frame and screen

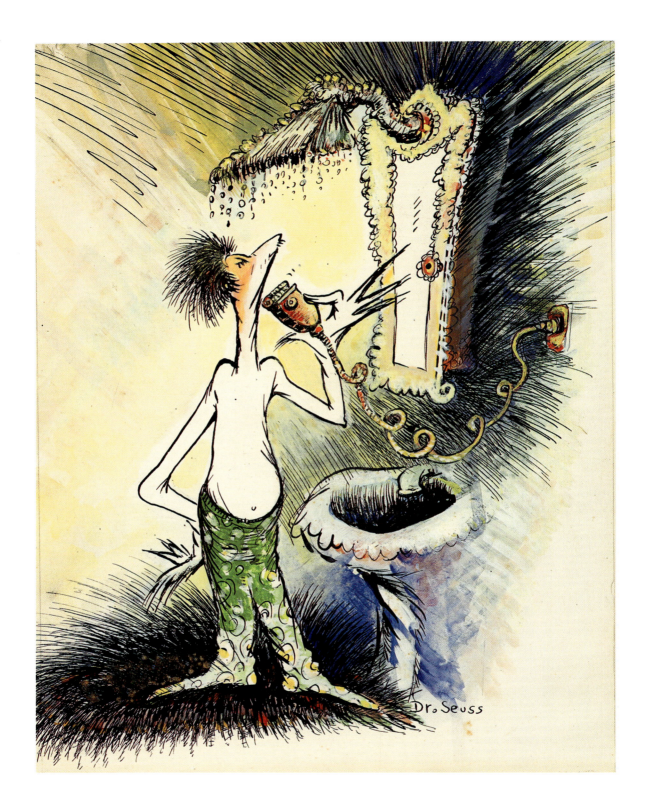

Self-Portrait as a Young Man Shaving 1964

dimensions 10⅝" x 8⅜"
media Ink and watercolor on board

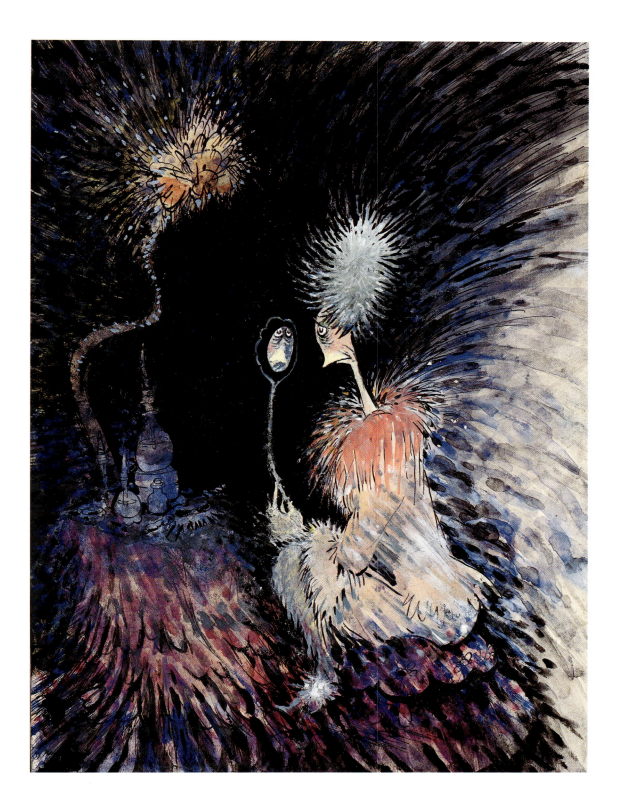

Gosh!, Do I Look as Old as all *That*! 1961

dimensions 12⅞" x 9½"
media Ink and watercolor on board

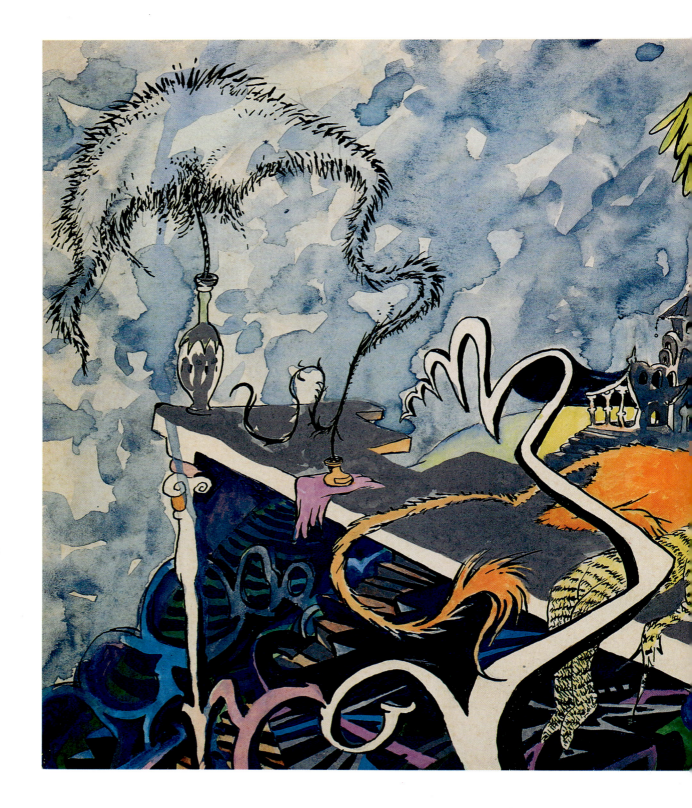

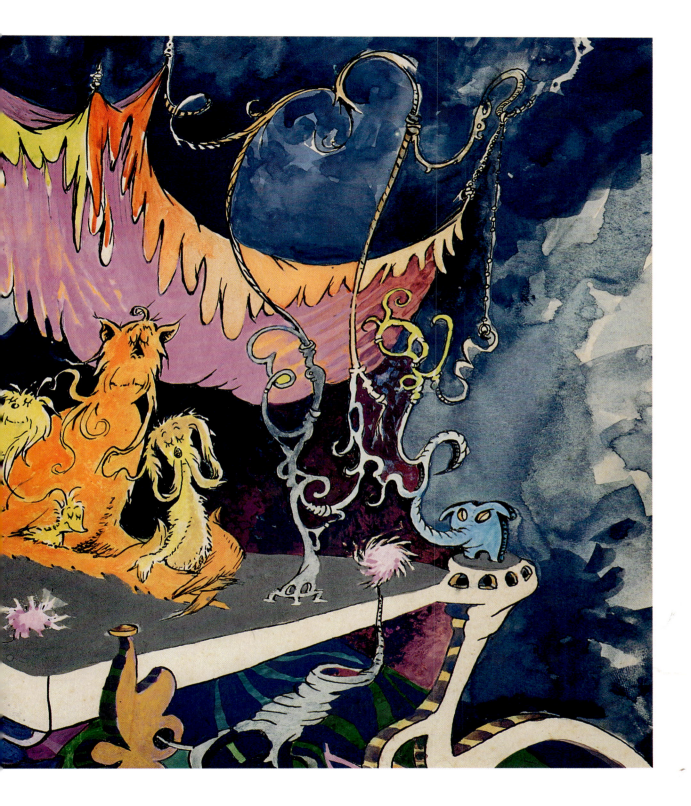

Relaxed in Spite of It

dimensions 9" x 16⅛"
media Pen and ink, watercolor on illustration board

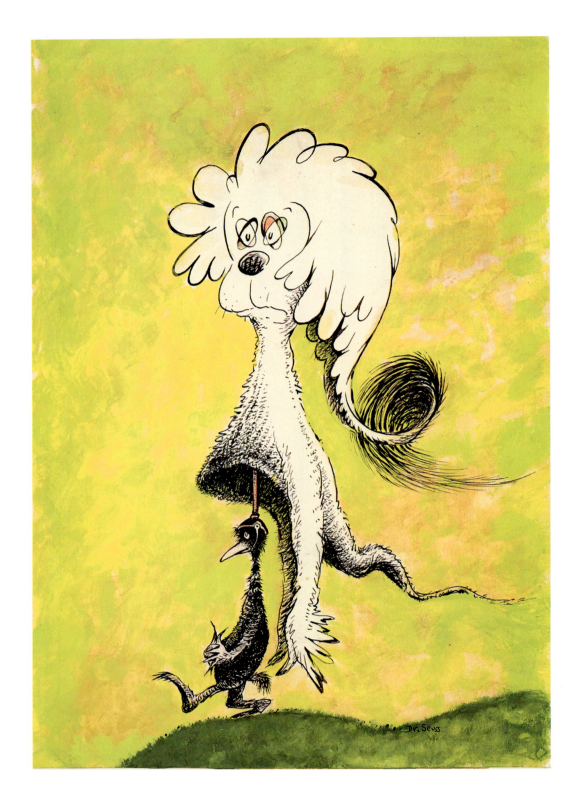

Fooling Nobody 1968

dimensions 14⅜" x 9¾"
media Ink and watercolor on bristol

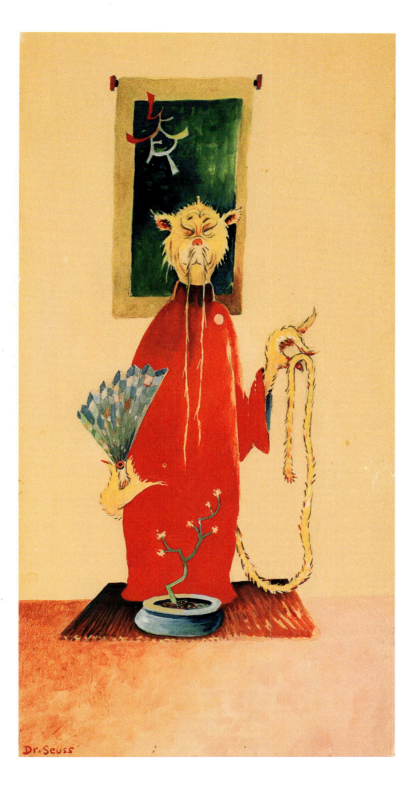

Wisdom of the Orient Cat 1964

dimensions 15⅜" x 7⅝"
media Oil on illustration board

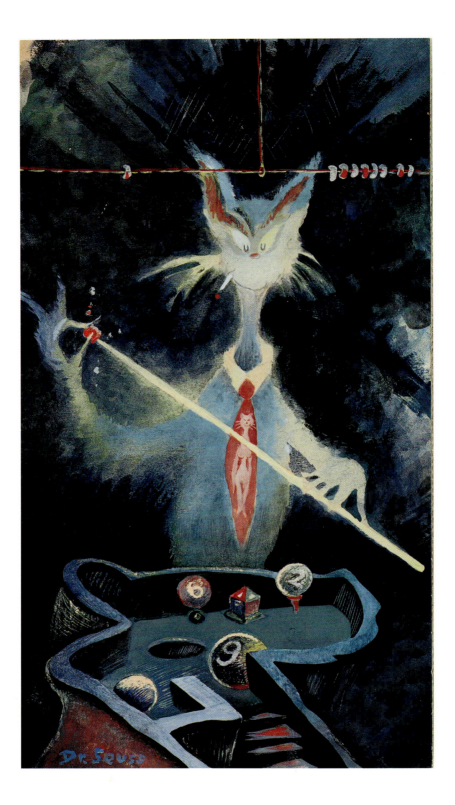

Cat from the Wrong Side of the Tracks 1964

dimensions 13" x 7"
media Oil on illustration board

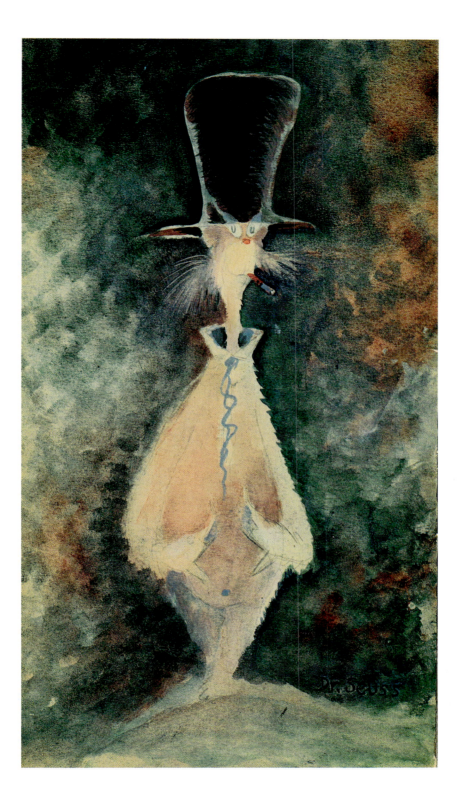

Indistinct Cat with Cigar

dimensions 13" x 7"
media Oil on illustration board

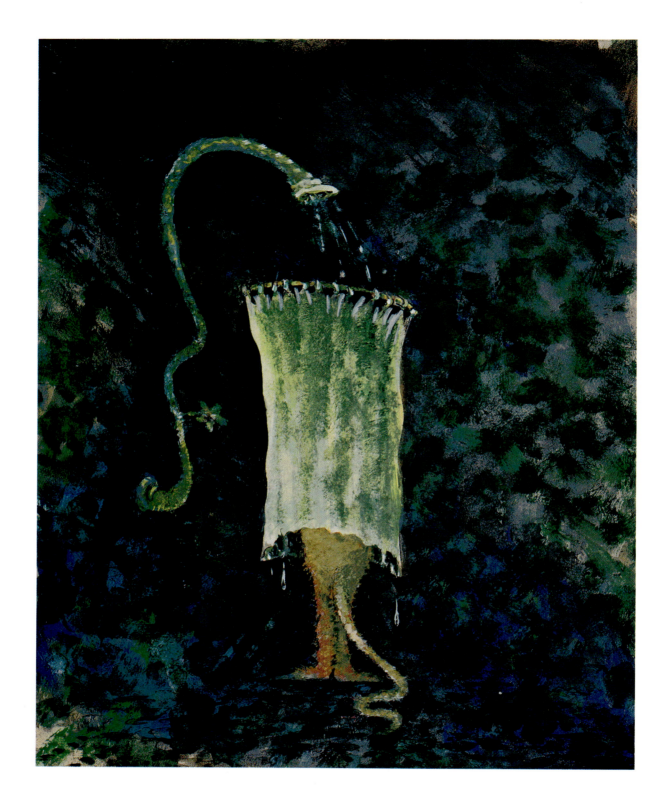

Cat in Obsolete Shower Bath (study)

dimensions 9¼" x 7½"
media Oil on bristol

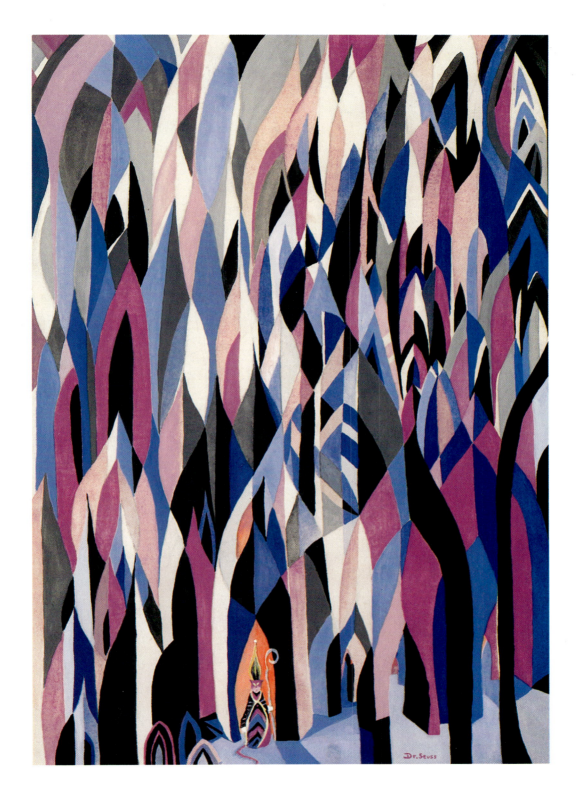

Archbishop Katz 1964

dimensions 20" x 16"
media Watercolor on illustration board

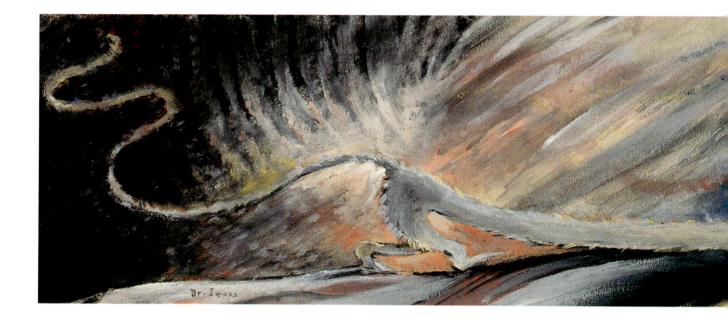

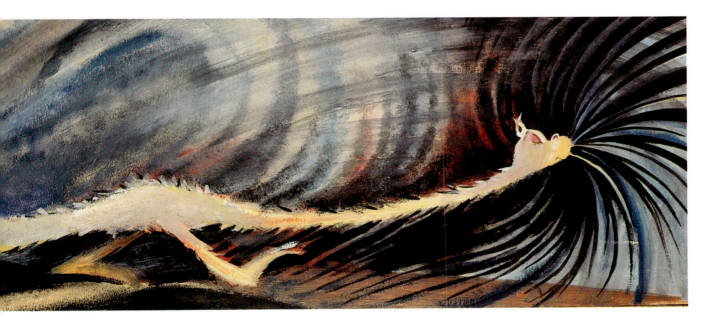

Alley Cat for a Very Long Alley 1964

dimensions 6⅛" x 28⅜"
media Acrylic and casein on Masonite

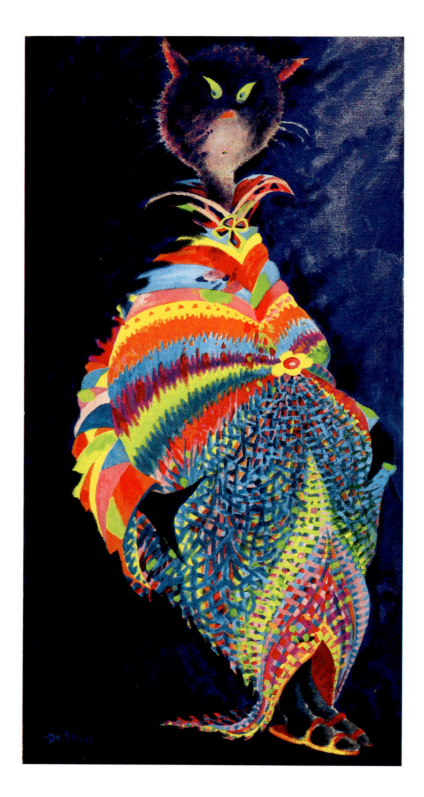

Joseph Katz and His Coat of Many Colors 1970

dimensions 20" x 10"
media Acrylic on canvas board

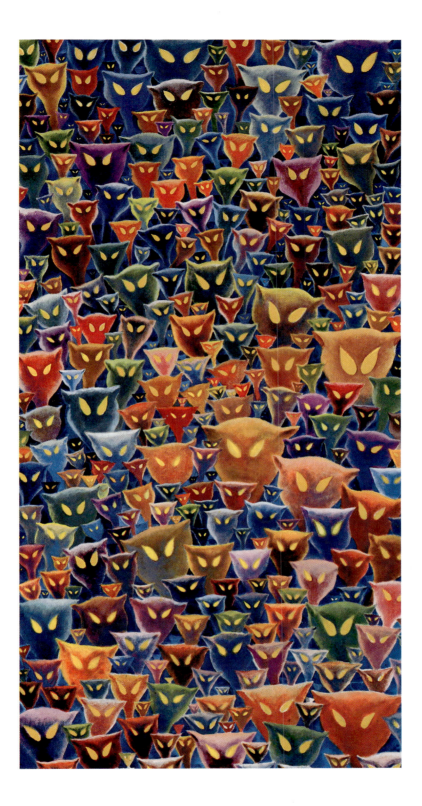

A Plethora of Cats 1970

dimensions 48" x 24"
media Oil on canvas

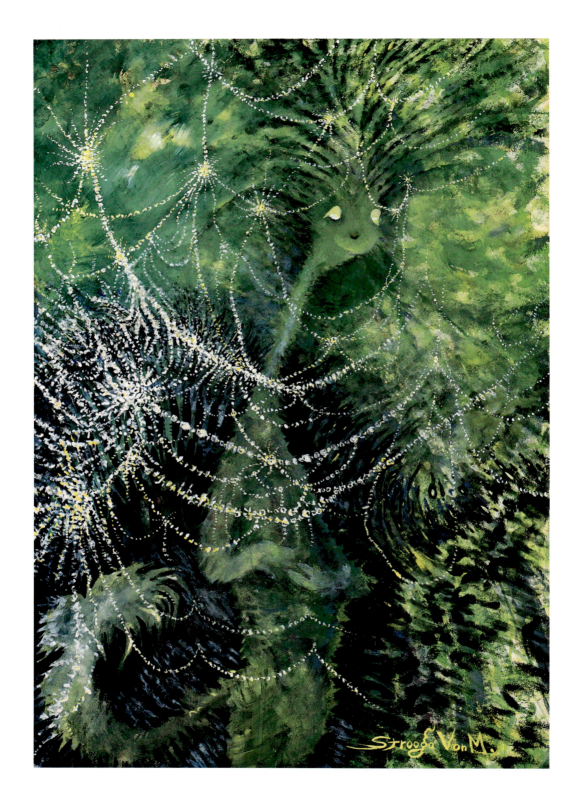

Green Cat with Lights

dimensions 16" x 10½"
media Oil on illustration board

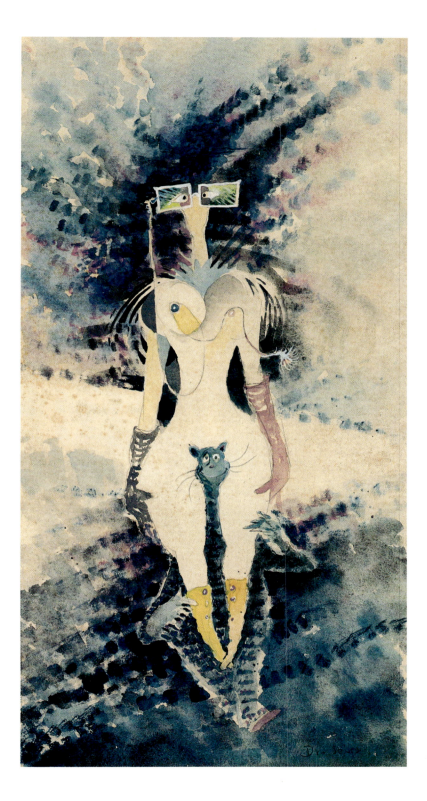

The Rather Odd Myopic Woman Riding Piggyback on One of Helen's Many Cats

dimensions 22⅜" x 14⅜"
media Pencil and watercolor on illustration board

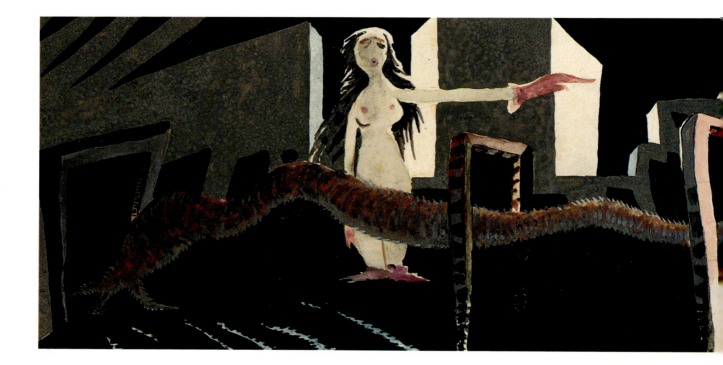

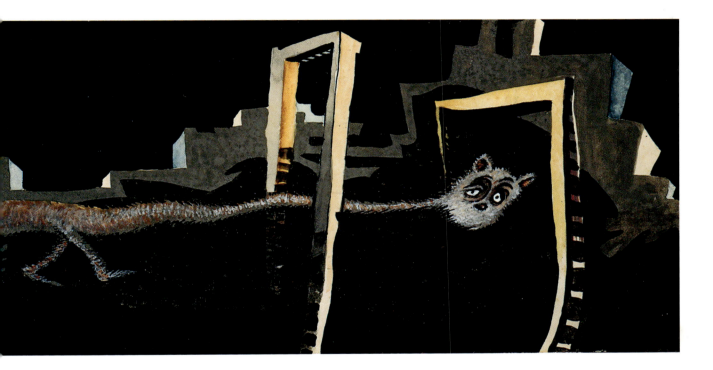

Surly Cat Being Ejected

dimensions 4¼" x 17"
media Gouache and enamel on illustration board

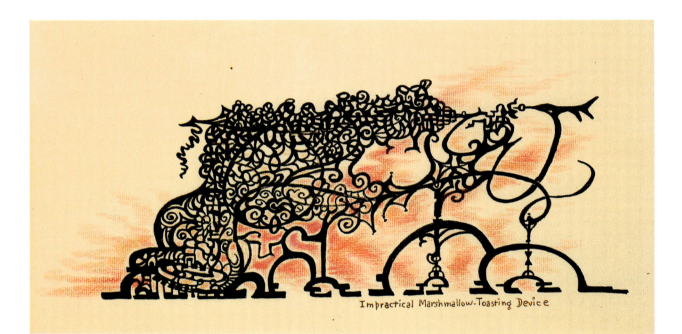

Impractical Marshmallow-Toasting Device

Impractical Marshmallow-Toasting Device

dimensions 12" x 17¾"
media Ink and crayon on paper

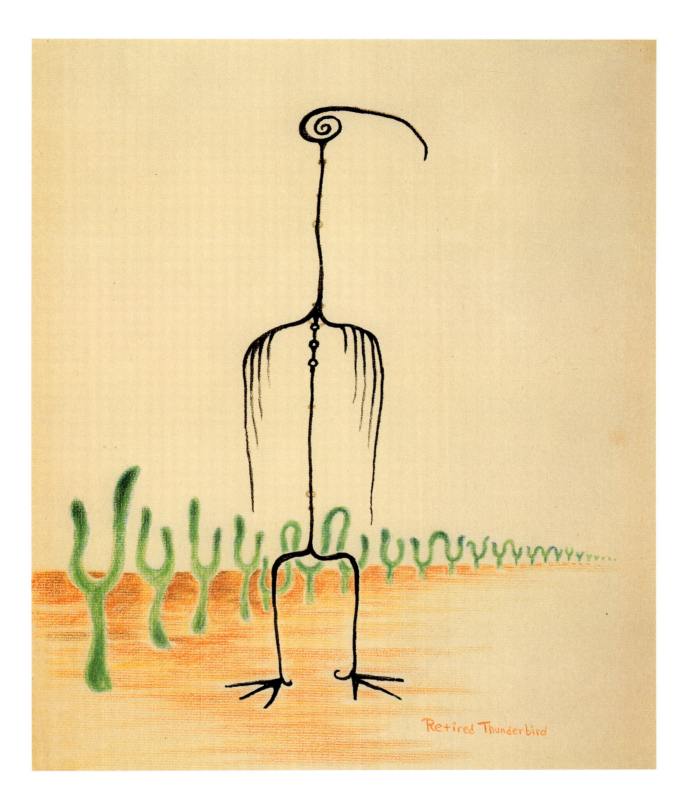

Retired Thunderbird

dimensions 14½" x 12"
media Ink and crayon on paper

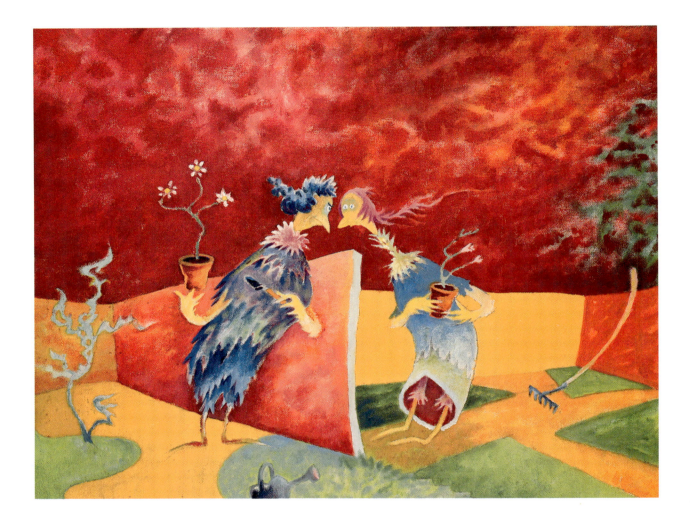

My Petunia Can Lick Your Geranium

dimensions 16" x 20"
media Acrylic on canvas board

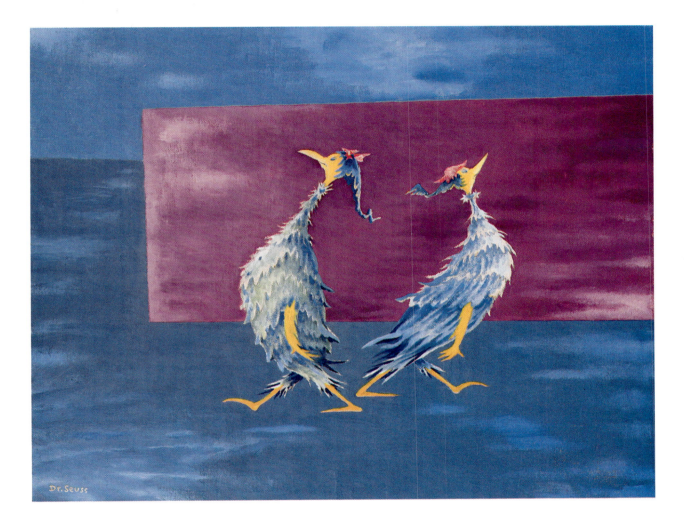

Not Speaking

dimensions 16" x 20"
media Oil on canvas board

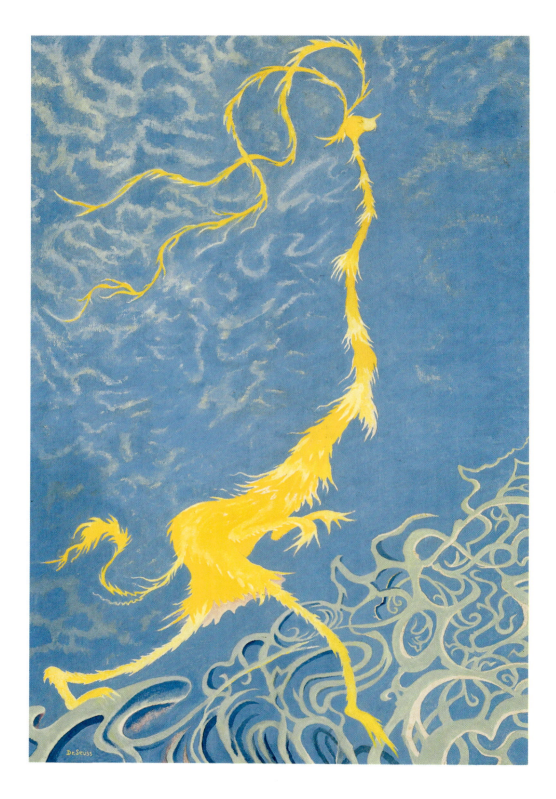

Golden Girl

dimensions 24" x 36"
media Oil on canvas board

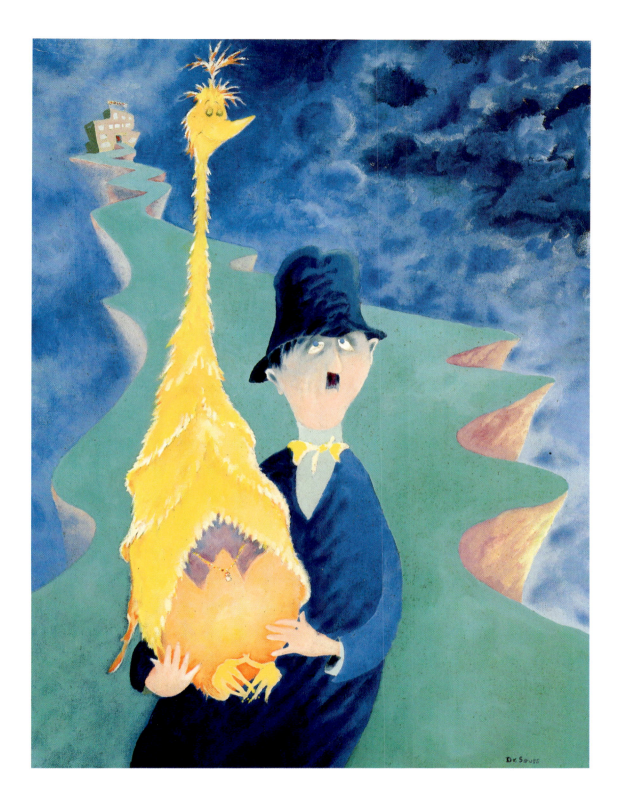

A Man Who Has Made an Unwise Prochess (*sic*) 1967

dimensions 24" x 18"
media Oil on canvas board

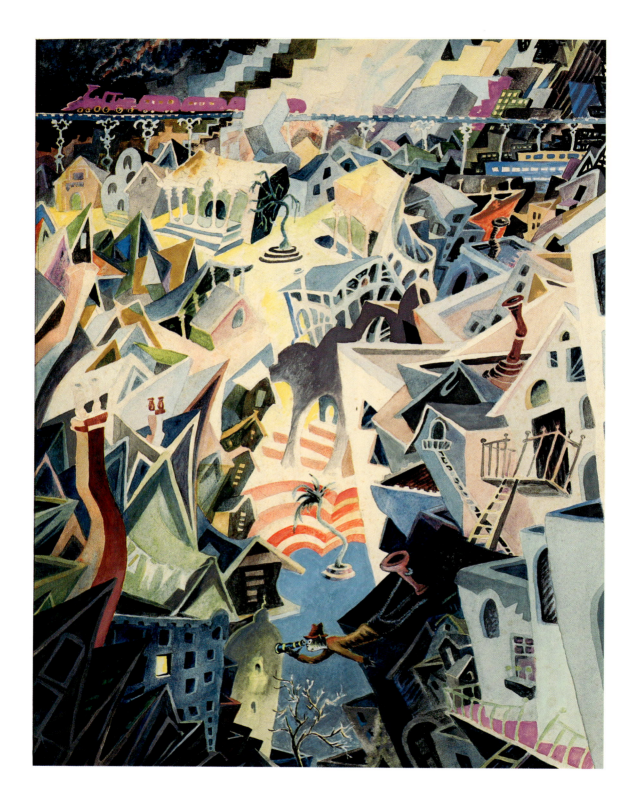

68

Cat Detective in the Wrong Part of Town 1969

dimensions 19½" x 14¼"
media Watercolor and pencil on illustration board

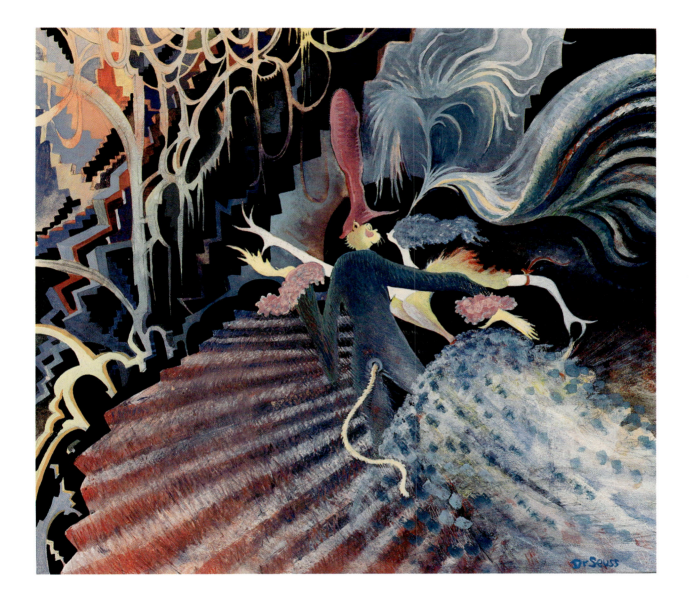

Cat Carnival in West Venice

dimensions 14¼" x 15½"
media Watercolor and pencil on board

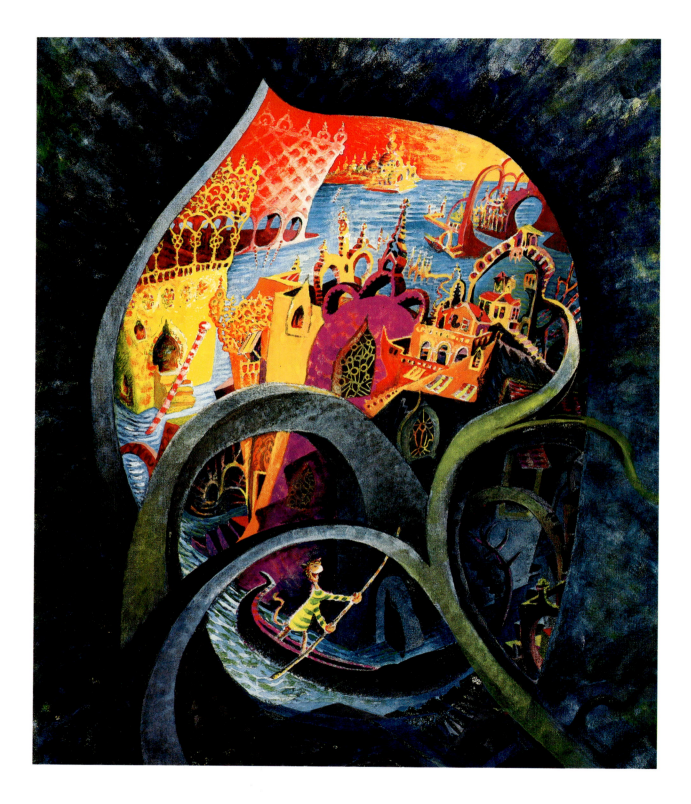

Venetian Cat-Singing Oh Solo Meow 1967

dimensions 23½" x 19½"
media Oil on canvas board

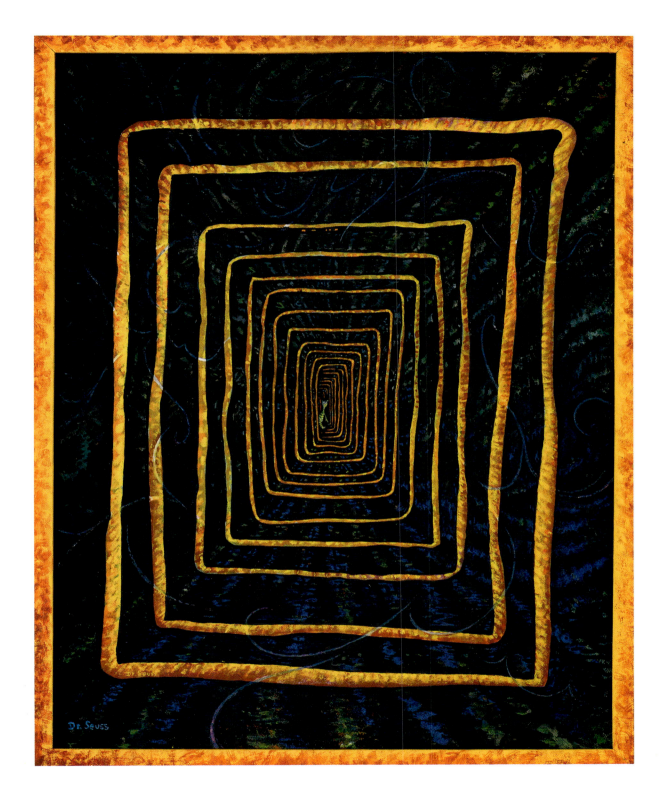

Green Cat in Uleabourge Finland Subway

dimensions 26⅜" x 20¾"
media Acrylic on illustration board and wood frame

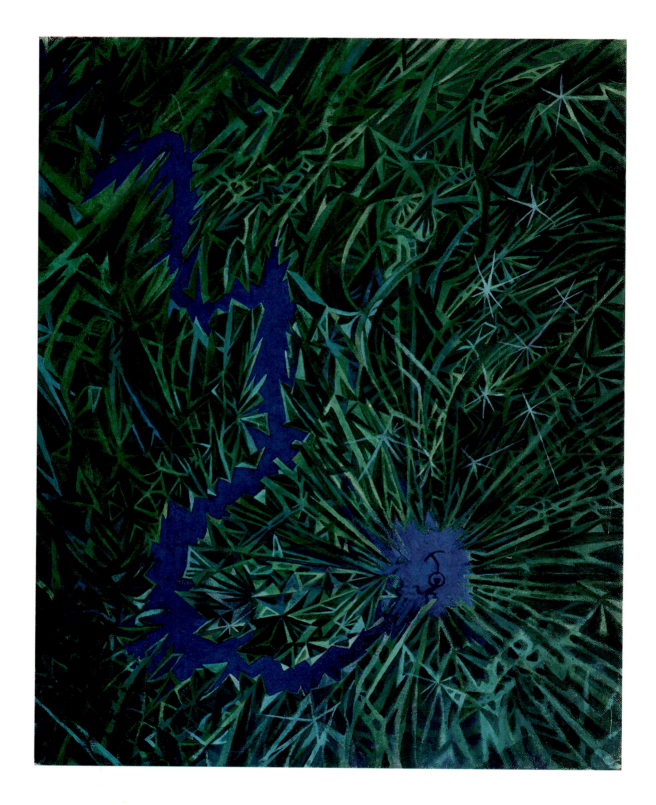

Minor-Cat Miner in a High-Yield Emerald Mine

dimensions 17⅞" x 13⅞"
media Acrylic and casein on canvas board

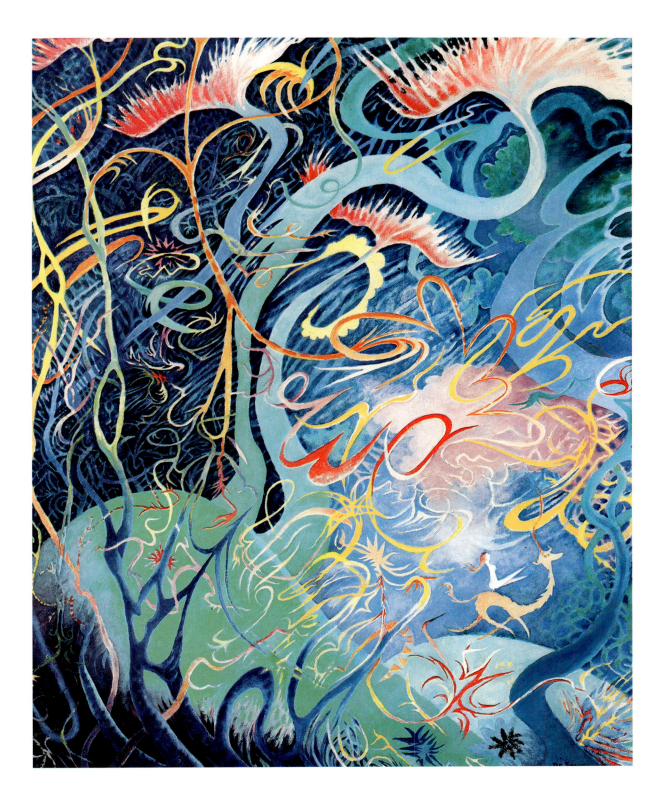

A Unicorn Every Girl Should Have

dimensions 29" x 23"
media Oil and pencil on board

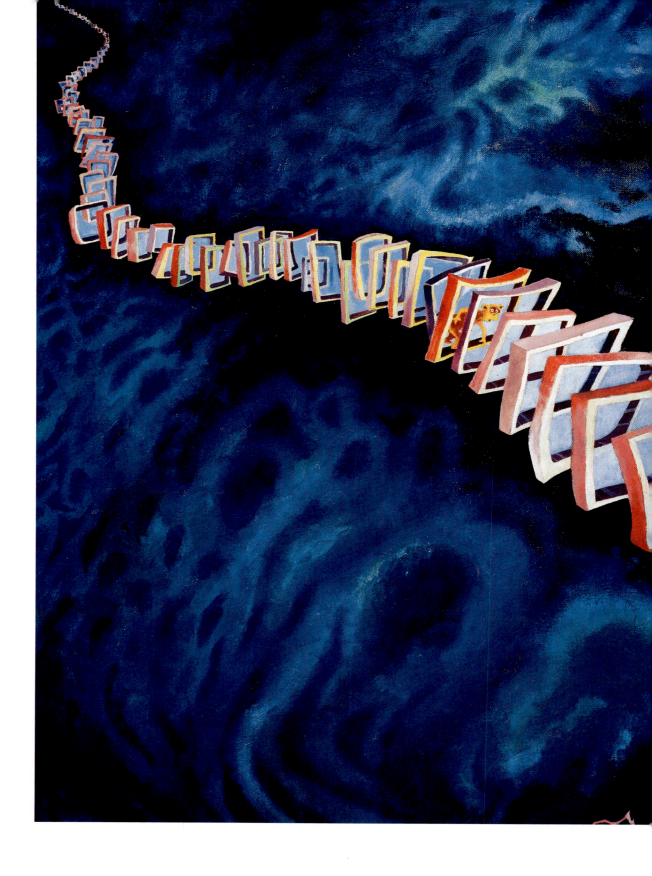

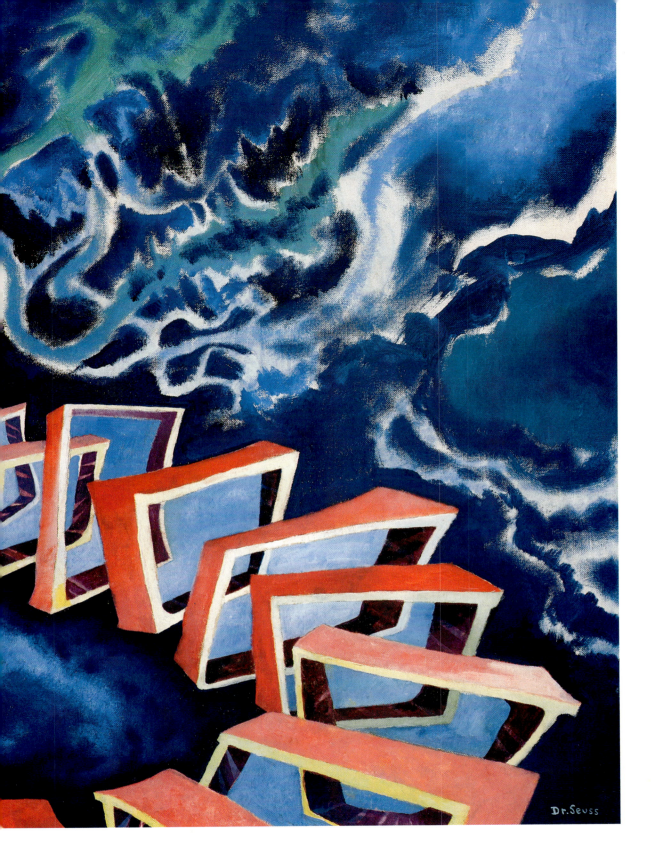

Untitled

dimensions 24" x 36"
media Oil on canvas board

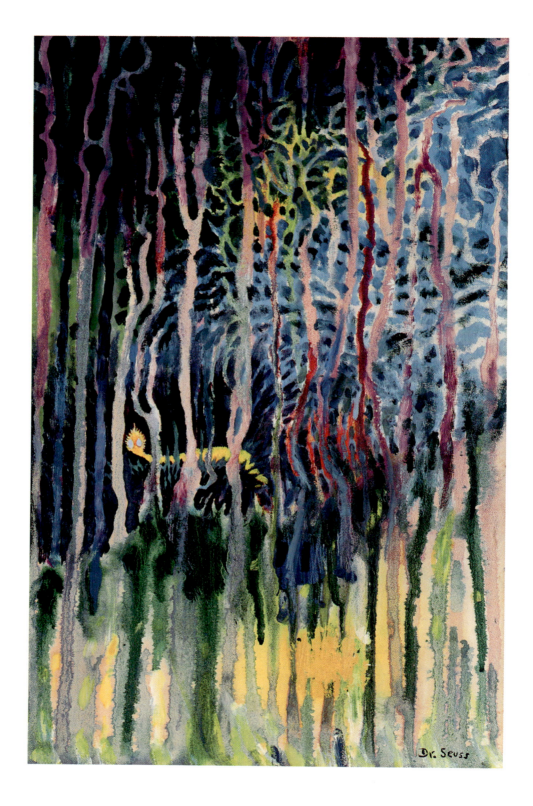

Worm Burning Bright in the Forest in the Night 1969

dimensions 15⅜" x 9⅝"
media Oil on illustration board

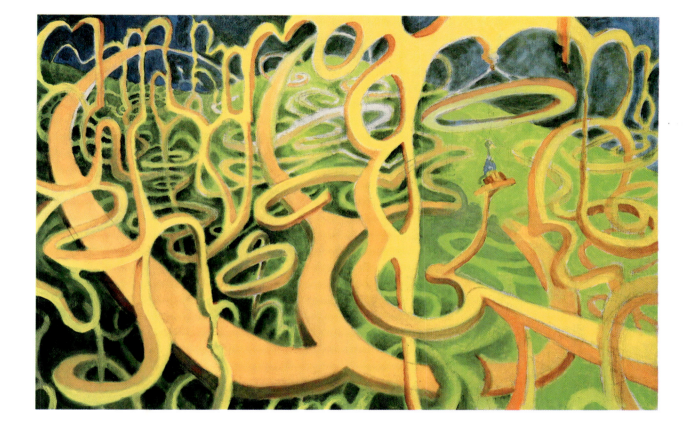

Intolerable Situation for a Cat

dimensions 24" x 36"
media Oil on canvas

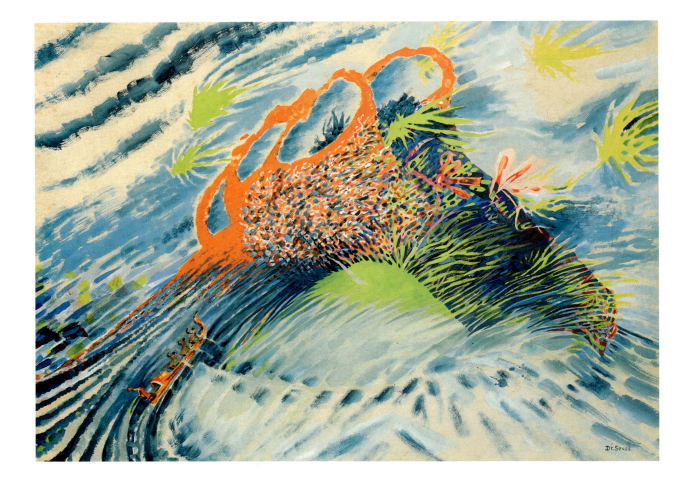

Untitled

dimensions 21⅞" x 29¾"
media Acrylic on illustration board

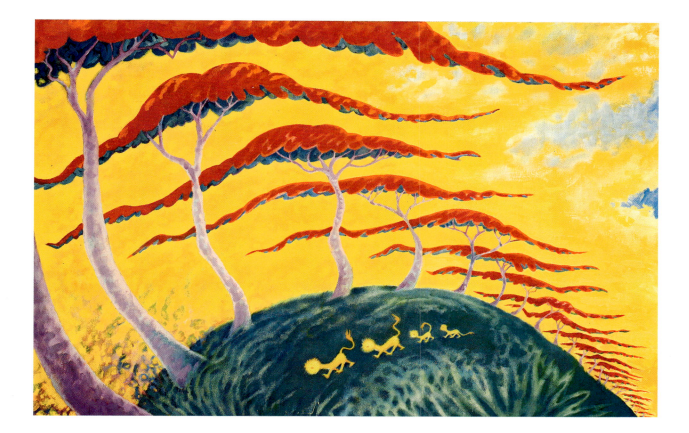

Lion Stroll

dimensions 24" x 36"
media Oil on canvas board

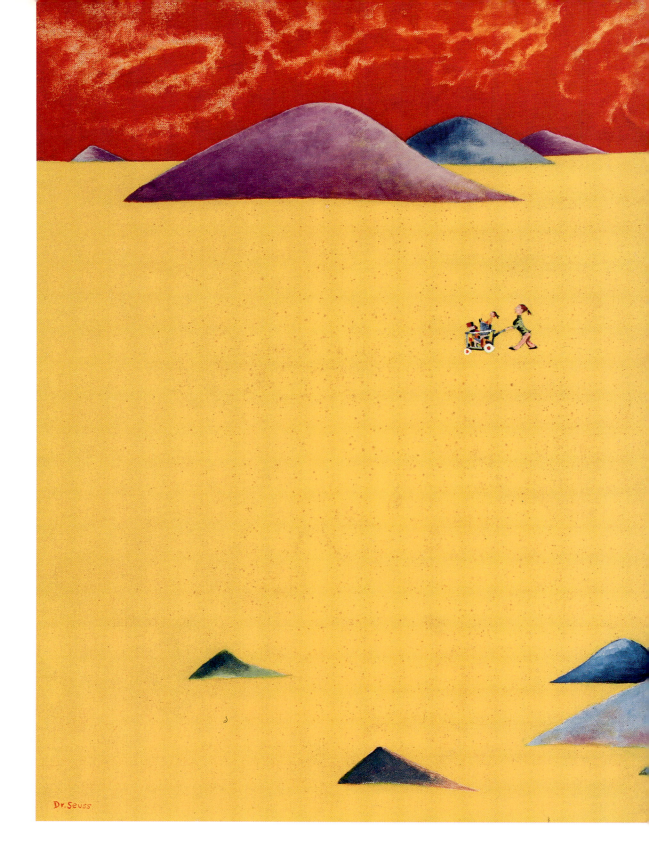

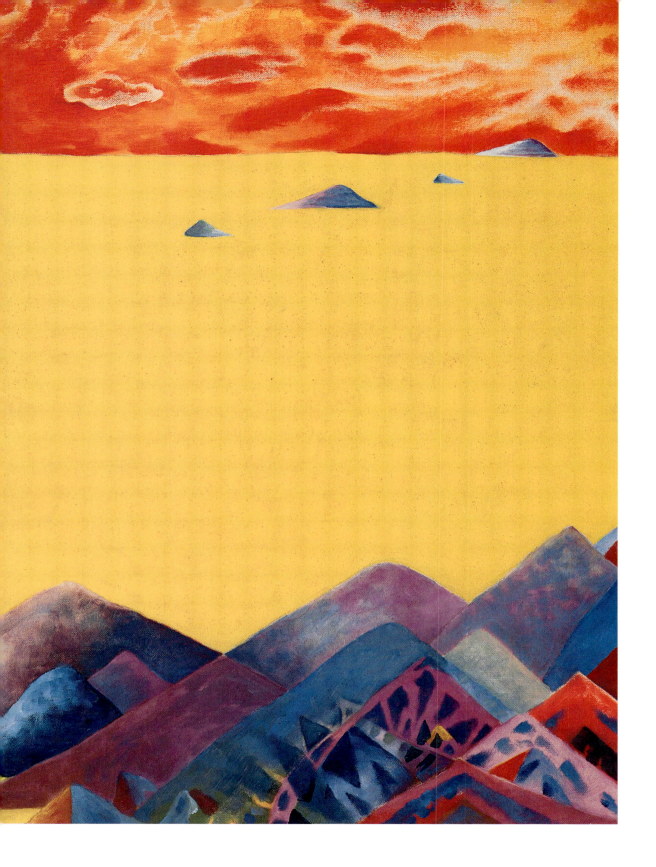

Western Woman

dimensions 24" x 36"
media Oil on canvas board

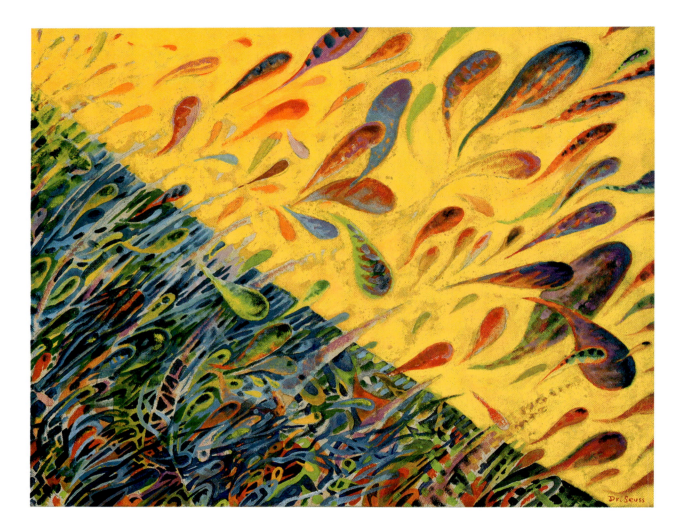

The Joyous Leaping of Uncanned Salmon

dimensions 15⅞" x 19"
media Acrylic on canvas board

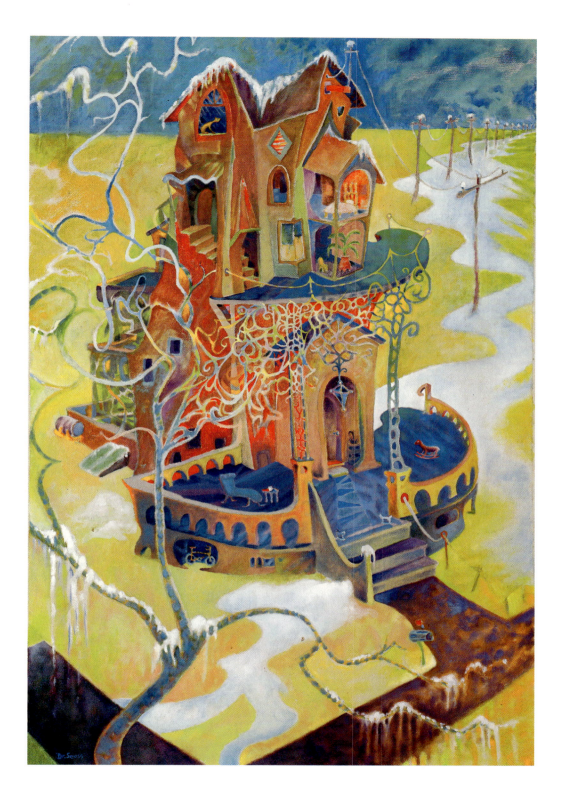

That Winter Spring Came Late 1969

dimensions 36" x 24"
media Oil on canvas board

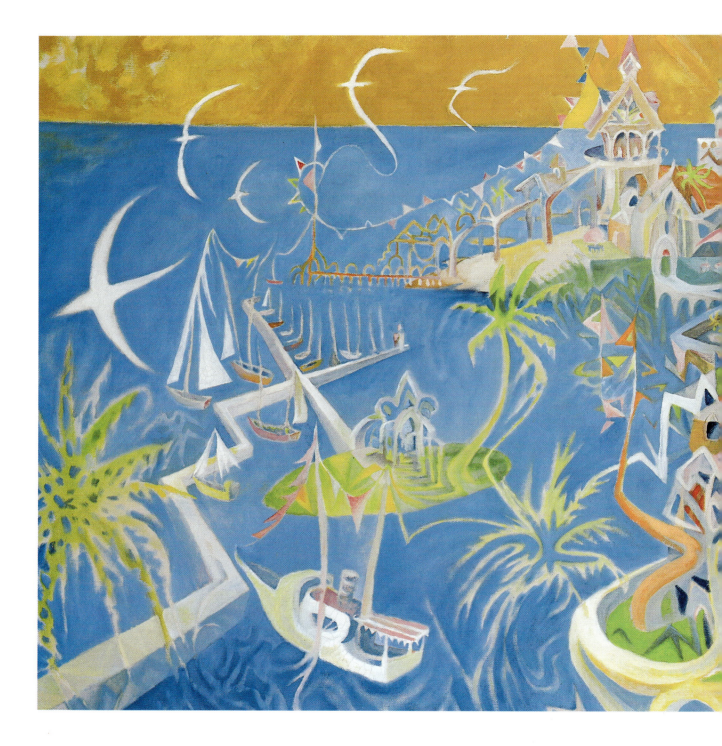

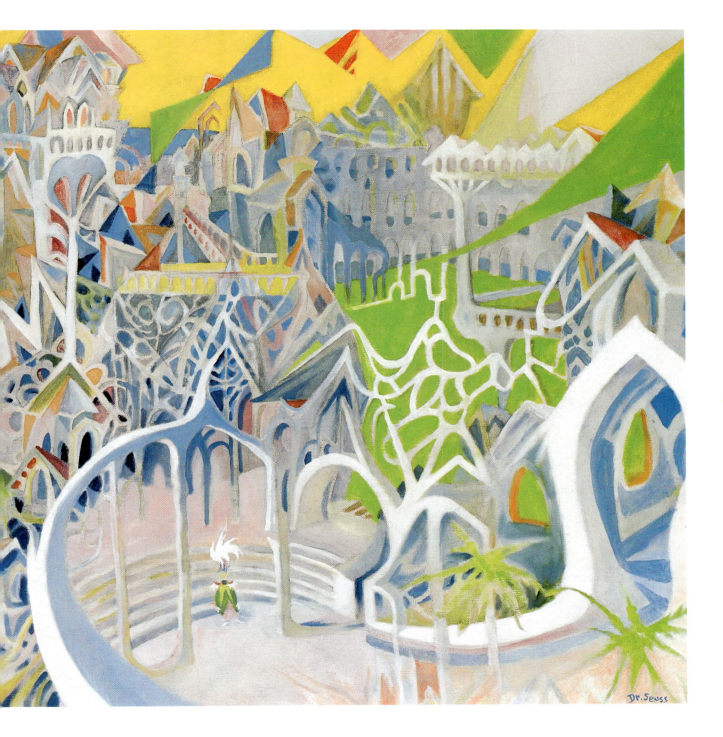

I Dreamed I Was a Doorman at the Hotel del Coronado 1970

dimensions 24" x 48"
media Acrylic on canvas

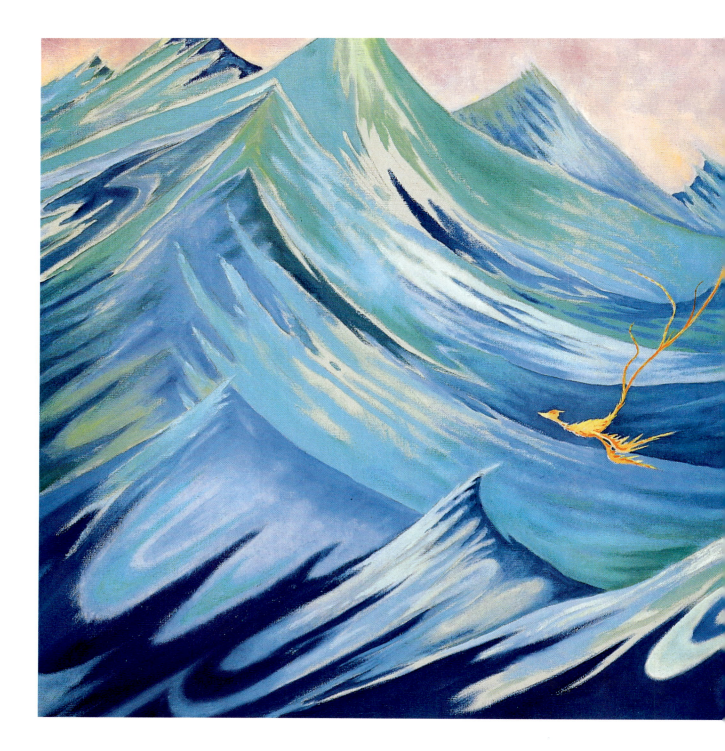

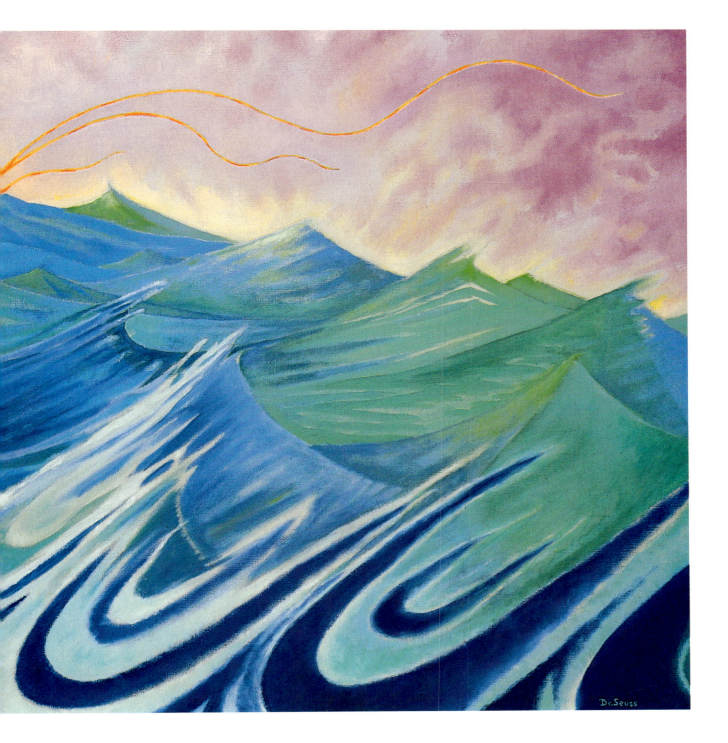

Untitled

dimensions 24" x 47¾"
media Oil on canvas

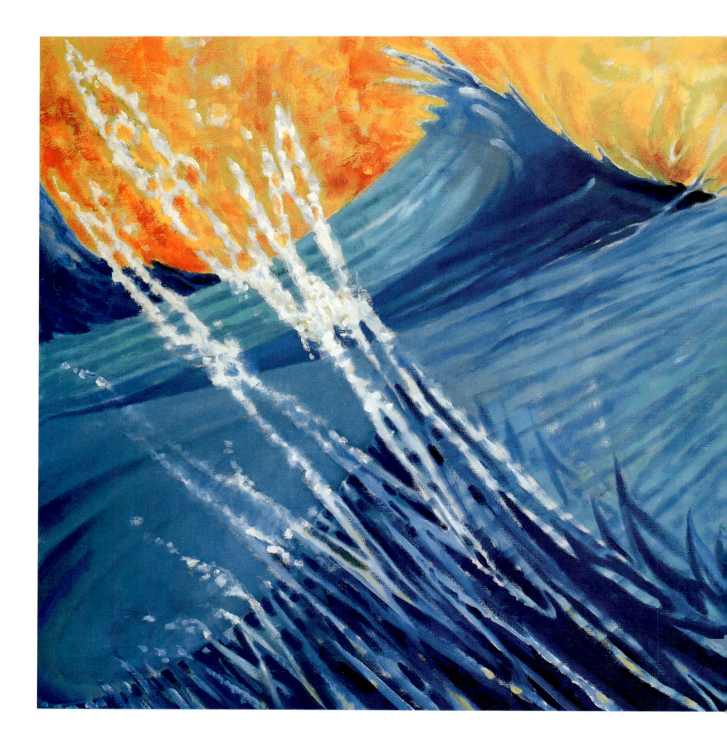

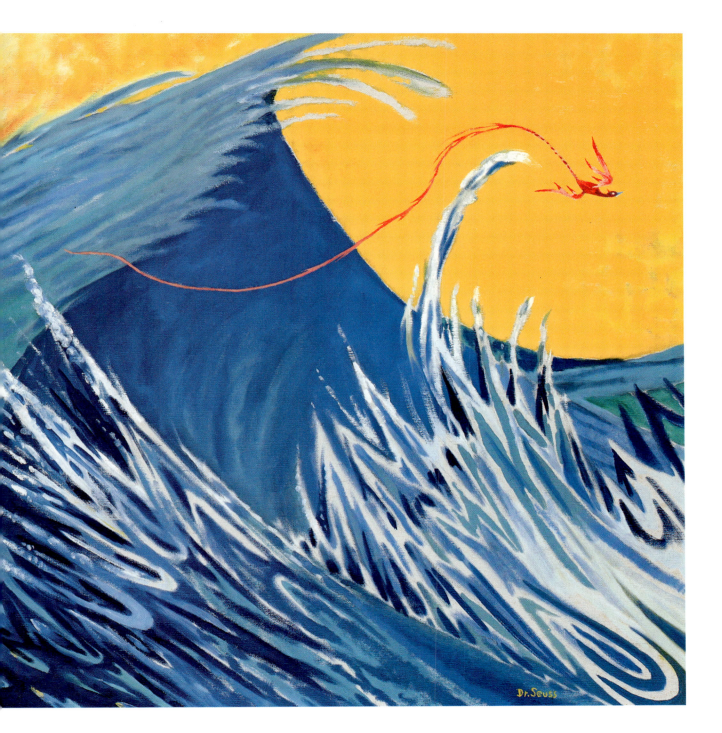

Untitled

dimensions 24" x 48"
media Oil on canvas

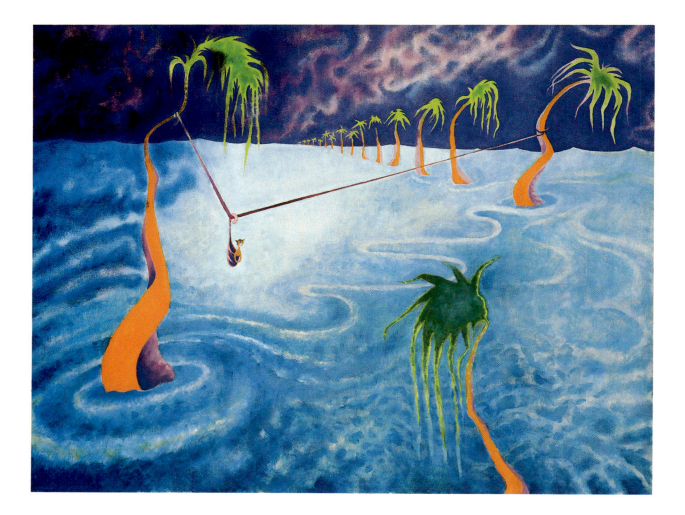

Lonely

dimensions 22" x 28"
media Acrylic on canvas board

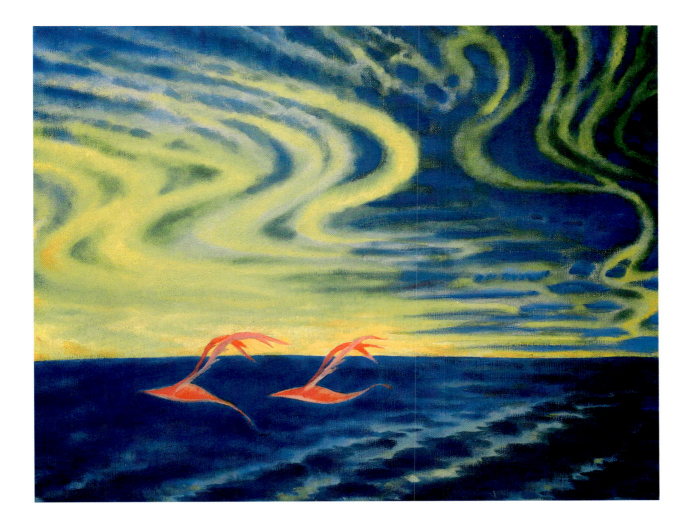

Untitled

dimensions 15⅞" x 20"
media Oil on canvas

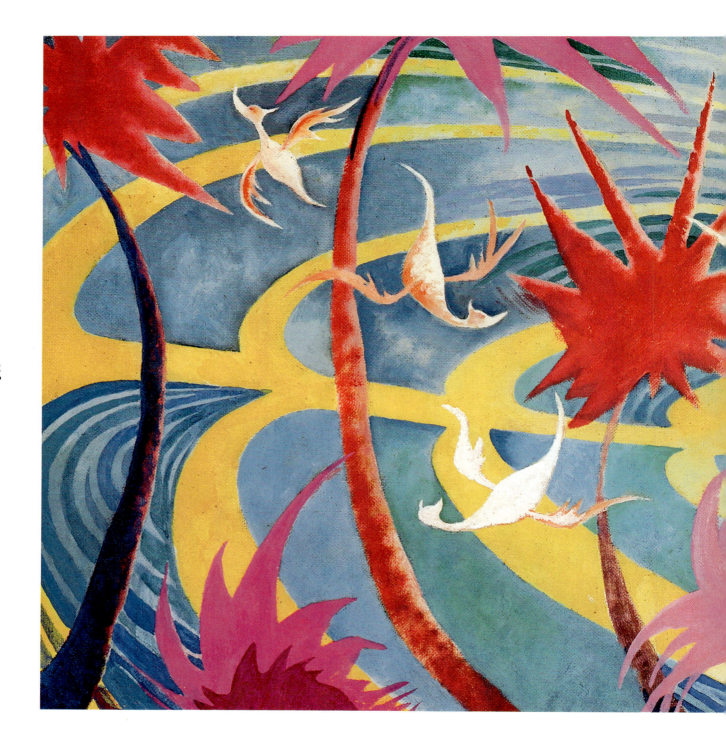

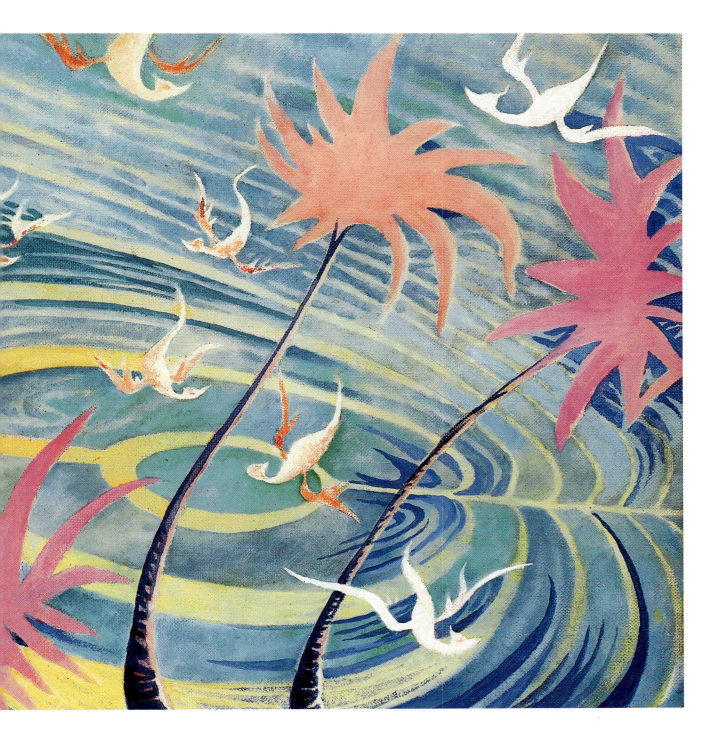

93

Tahitian Landscape 1966

dimensions 12" x 24"
media Acrylic on canvas board

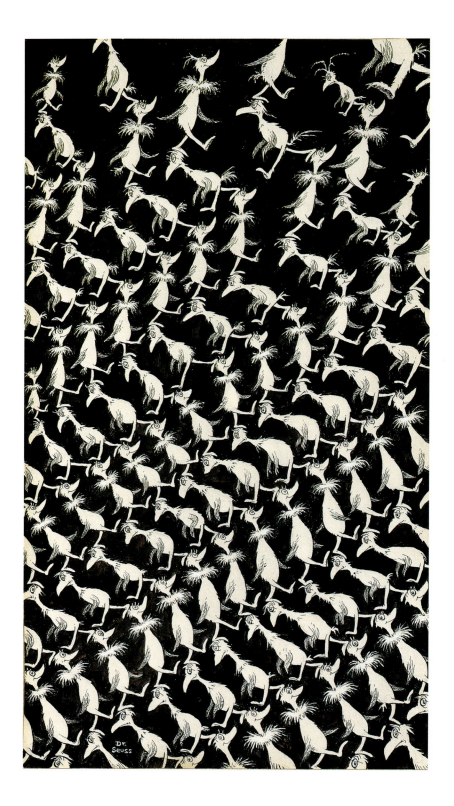

The Economic Situation Clarified 1975

dimensions 22½" x 11⅞"
media Ink on bristol

A Chronology of Books Written and Illustrated by Dr. Seuss

1937	And to Think That I Saw It on Mulberry Street
1937	The 500 Hats of Bartholomew Cubbins
1937	The Seven Lady Godivas
1939	The King's Stilts
1940	Horton Hatches the Egg
1947	McElligot's Pool
1948	Thidwick the Big-Hearted Moose
1949	Bartholomew and the Oobleck
1950	If I Ran the Zoo
1953	Scrambled Eggs Super!
1954	Horton Hears a Who!
1955	On Beyond Zebra!
1956	If I Ran the Circus
1957	The Cat in the Hat
1957	How the Grinch Stole Christmas!
1958	The Cat in the Hat Comes Back
1958	Yertle the Turtle and Other Stories
1959	Happy Birthday to You!
1960	Green Eggs and Ham
1960	One Fish Two Fish Red Fish Blue Fish
1961	The Sneetches and Other Stories
1962	Dr. Seuss's Sleep Book
1963	Dr. Seuss's ABC
1963	Hop on Pop
1965	Fox in Socks
1965	I Had Trouble in Getting to Solla Sollew
1967	The Cat in the Hat Songbook
1968	The Foot Book
1969	I Can Lick 30 Tigers Today! and Other Stories
1970	I Can Draw It Myself
1970	Mr. Brown Can Moo! Can You?
1971	The Lorax
1972	Marvin K. Mooney Will You Please Go Now!
1973	Did I Ever Tell You How Lucky You Are?
1973	The Shape of Me and Other Stuff
1974	There's a Wocket in My Pocket!
1975	Oh, the Thinks You Can Think!
1976	The Cat's Quizzer
1978	I Can Read with My Eyes Shut!
1979	Oh Say Can You Say?
1982	Hunches in Bunches
1984	The Butter Battle Book
1986	You're Only Old Once!
1990	Oh, the Places You'll Go!
1991	Six by Seuss